Speaking **Naturally**

Your Guide To Confident Successful Public Speaking

Published by the Wellness Institute, Inc., 1007 Whitney Ave.
Gretna, LA 70056, August 1, 2002.

Cover design by the Wellness Institute, Inc.
Selfhelpbooks.com is a division of the

Wellness Institute, Inc.
Gretna, LA 70056

ISBN: 1-58741-121-0
Printed in the United States of America.

Speaking **Naturally**

Your Guide To Confident Successful Public Speaking

Sean F. Kelly, Ph.D.
and
Reid J. Kelly, A.C.S.W.

I love natural, simple and unaffected speech…
Montaigne

Table of Contents

DEDICATION

For Amy and Ian

Chapter One

Speaking Naturally

Talking is natural. It really is.

Most children have begun to speak by the time they are two years old. Within months they have developed large working vocabularies and the essentials of grammar. They are able to voice ideas, needs, and wishes. While it may be called a miracle, the ability to speak is an everyday one.

That is, talking is natural unless it means giving "a talk."

For many people, getting up in front of an audience to speak is a nightmare, often beginning days before the actual talk. Anxiety mounts. The mouth goes dry, the palms become moist, and the armpits are soaked. Hands tremble, knees knock, and the voice, once steady and confident, becomes high, quavering, soft and fast. And then there is the blushing. And the stammering. And the absolutely blank mind. A once natural act of communication has been transformed into an ordeal, just as the benevolent Doctor Jeckyll changed into the malevolent Mister Hyde.

Saying your name is natural. Or it is until you are sitting in a circle as people introduce themselves. That's when you might find yourself anxiously awaiting your turn. You mentally rehearse identifying yourself, as though you might draw a blank when your time comes.

Even when fear is not an issue, getting up to speak persuasively and coherently can be quite a task. Ideas jumble, the audience has trouble following your train of thought, and there is too much talk for too little time.

People who know a subject in great depth sometimes have trouble communicating their knowledge to others precisely because they know so much. People asked to speak on a subject about which they have limited knowledge tend to focus on these limits and therefore radiate incompetence.

Some find an audience of strangers intimidating; others find co-workers worse. Presenting to bosses or in the presence of supervisors has a special degree of challenge. How do you sound coherent when half the people are familiar with your topic, half know nothing, and all are in the audience listening to you? Suppose they are hostile? Or bored? Or they know more than you?

Then there are the issues of audience size, sitting or standing to talk, speaking formally or informally, standing behind a podium or walking around, using notes, PowerPoint, handouts, or overheads, and speaking alone or as part of a team. And then there are your hands. Where on earth are they supposed to go? And suppose you get asked a question you cannot answer. Or you ask the audience a question and nobody answers. How ever did Dante overlook the Circle of Presentations in *The Inferno*?

Also, the process of preparing a presentation can be a lengthy one for many people. Even someone who might enjoy giving the speech might find the required investment of time and energy to be so great, interfering so much with all other work, that the preparation becomes an odious task. This need for hours of preparation makes the prospect of an impromptu talk daunting at best and completely impossible for many.

Getting up to read someone else' work in public can feel like a rerun of the third grade, with anxiety and stress interfering with your ability to perform the simple task of reading. You know how to read without even thinking about it, but standing up and doing so seems a Labor of Hercules, even though the words are all there in black and white. Maybe you can read only when you do not think about it.

What on earth is going on?

Slow down. Take it easy. You can do this. Or, rather, you will be able to do it.

This book is a journey of discovery, where you will learn what it takes to present clearly, confidently, comfortably, and persuasively. For many would-be speakers it seems to be an impossible task. You might think that you cannot learn to do this because you have failed in the past. You might attribute it to forces beyond your control. Perhaps you believe that you were born shy, that you lack the skill set of a powerful speaker, or simply that the task is too great. For whatever reason, it may feel out of your hands. But the real problem is that you do not know how to go about learning to become an excellent speaker.

Note that the goal is to be an excellent speaker. It is not merely to achieve the level of mediocrity. In fact, low expectations lead to low achievements. If your goal is to become minimally competent, then that is the absolute best you may achieve. Telling yourself that you will never be too good makes it unlikely you will even be average. Aiming low is a set-up for doing even worse.

The goal of this book is excellence. You can and will learn to be the best speaker you can be. You will not get a new voice, body, history, or memory. You will still be you. But you will be able to learn new skills and techniques to make the most of what you already have.

As you proceed through this book, you will learn to do things one step at a time. The size of each step will be not more than you can handle. You will get directions that will allow you to succeed. Problems will be taken apart so you can learn to do that which seems impossible at first glance. For example, if you were told to increase your heart rate, you might well say that it was impossible, that you do not know how to do so, that nobody can tell his or her heart to speed up. However, if you were instructed to stand up and begin to do aerobic exercises (or, perhaps, to get up and deliver a speech!) your heartbeat would indeed speed up. So it is not a matter of being unable to do it, but rather of not knowing how to do it, of needing to learn how to do it, particularly when the mechanism is not apparent. You are going to learn the elements that make up the ability to speak in public, whether to an audience of one or one thousand. You will learn to make talking natural again.

Keep in mind that what you are doing is returning to a normal and natural thing to do. Remembering this will simplify the task.

Because it is easy to think of talking in public as something hard to do, examples are taken from a wide variety of sources to help break the mold of that mindset. Stories about humans and animals are used to demonstrate points. Metaphors are employed extensively to make learning more intuitive. The reasons behind problems will be examined and understood. You will learn parables and visual images to make it easy to apply the skills you acquire.

Those who already love speaking will learn techniques to improve their ability. Those who dread it will learn to overcome their dislikes or and fears. This book can enable you to make the improvements you wish to make.

The goal of this book is not to teach you how to endure public speaking or how to tolerate the anxiety and discomfort of presenting. It is to teach you to enjoy speaking clearly, comfortably, and persuasively. The goal is Excellence.

It will return you to your original state, where talking is natural, even in front of an audience.

Chapter Two

The Decision Is Yours

"This book can enable you to make the improvements you wish to make."

That sentence near the end of Chapter One is easy to glide over or even miss completely, but it is absolutely vital that you give it the attention it deserves. This book *can* teach you, but only if you want to learn.

The first step has to be desire. You have to decide you want to learn to do this. This is a choice.

Before you start trying to learn to do anything, you first must decide whether you want to do it or not. Not whether your boss, or your spouse, or your mother, or your mentor, or anyone else wants you to do it, but whether you want to do it. And the question is not whether your job demands it, or you ought to be able to do it, or everyone else does it, or people in your position do it, or whether you know you have to learn to do it, but whether you choose to learn.

People learn only when they want to learn and only what they want to learn. You need to decide whether you really want to learn to be a speaker. How to do it only makes sense after you have made the decision you want to do it. It is pointless to figure out how to get to Khartoum until you have decided you actually want to visit Central Africa.

If you do not want to do something, your motivation will be against doing it. You will be motivated only to fail. How hard will you really work at something when success would result in your having to continue to do something you hate? People who hate flying are not tempted by Frequent Flier Miles that offer the prospect of extra trips. People who hate sports are not thrilled by overtime. When your heart is not in it, you will make excuses, often valid ones, and will find failure to be not so bitter.

When "No, I will not," is not an option, "I can't," often takes its place. A person who truly does not want to stop smoking cigarettes may try to mollify others by going through the motions of trying to stop, but ultimately he will continue to smoke, because that is what he wants to do. Rather than say he does not want to stop, he says he cannot.

Someone who does not want to get up in public to present is motivated to do a bad job. When forced to do so, the best option is to do badly. Despite all protestations of willingness "to give it a try," anyone would be self-sabotaging, because doing a good job will result in being asked to do it again.

This needs to be made explicit from the start. It is okay to decide you do not want to give talks.

Life is a series of options. Many of the things we do involve choices made. People decide where they want to live. They decide whether to get married, play tennis, wear sunscreen, have children, read magazines, contribute to the United Way, or get a puppy. There is nothing inherently wrong with choosing for or against any of these options. While it is not okay to be an ax murderer or to torture kittens, there are a great many acceptable options in life.

People work at a great many different types of jobs. Some require a suit and tie. Others require a bathing suit. Still others a blue collar. Some jobs require long hours; others have clearly defined eight-hour workdays. There are jobs that require public speaking and there are plenty of jobs where one is not permitted, much less forced, to speak in public. The options are myriad.

It is important that a person has a good fit between expectation and willingness. If you are not willing to work long hours, you will not be happy with a job that demands lots of overtime. Some people enjoy sales while others hate selling. The former might be happy working as a sales rep, but the latter should certainly look for a different line of work. The problem is not that there are good and bad jobs. Problems arise when a person and a lifestyle do not fit each other well. A job that demands travel is good if you want to see different places, but bad if being home for supper every night is important.

If you prefer a life that does not involve speaking in public, that is fine. You should get a job where speaking is not among the duties, just as you should get a job that allows casual dress if you don't want to wear a tie. And if you do not want to give talks, don't take volunteer positions or join groups where you would have to give talks. It is an acceptable choice. No one can make you give talks.

On the other hand, choosing to be in a situation where talking publicly is part of the package does not have to mean that it is the best part of the job. Every job has some elements that are good and others that are just part of the deal. You do not have to love your commute to work outside the home, just be willing to accept it. You do not have to live for the opportunity to give talks, but they should not be an onerous or dreaded task.

The attitude of the successful presenter is not "I have to give a talk." That would make anyone feel coerced into doing something against one's will. Instead, he or she thinks " I get to give a talk. I have the opportunity to get up in front of a group of powerful people and command their attention. It is a chance to shine, to stand out, to persuade, and to advance towards promotion."

The way we name something, the language we use to describe it, changes it in our minds. Think of the difference it makes if you describe someone as ancient or mature, an authority or a know-it-all, an intellectual or an egghead, compassionate or a bleeding heart. The name we give something affects how we feel about it. Calling presenting an opportunity rather than a curse makes a difference. Now it is something you are doing out of choice. Now you desire to learn to do it.

From the Kentucky Derby to rural fairgrounds, horse racing is the Sport of Kings. And while the owner, trainer, jockey, and bettors all hope for their horse to win, the essential excitement derives from the horses' own desire to win. For good horses, the urge to cross the finish line first is instinctive.

In the wild, horses naturally form herds. At the front of the herd runs its leader, the alpha horse. To be in front of the herd is to be the chief, the stallion who breeds with the mares. The front of the pack is the coveted position for horses. The best horses want to be out in front, so, when they race, the good horses compete to be first.

Not all horses are natural leaders who want to be in front. Some prefer to be in second or third place. They are the horses who challenge the best horses but never quite surpass them. They want to be lieutenants, not captains, the sidekicks, not the heroes. Ordinarily, they seem like good horses who are just not quite fast enough, but under special circumstances their nature is exposed.

Handicappers sometimes organize a Maiden race for horses who have never won. Some of the entrants may be running for the first time; others may have been racing against superior competition and are seeking their proper level. Some, though, might be horses who do not like to be in front, who are followers, not leaders. If all the entrants in a Maiden race are followers, the results can be hilarious.

All the horses break out of their gates and run in a pack. Some unfortunate horse notices that he is in front and is frightened by the exposure. He slows down and allows the pack to surround him. The result is that the poor horse who had been happy in second place now has been put in the lead. He too will put on the brakes to re-gain the safety of the herd. The race continues like a sort of reverse musical chairs, with horses struggling to get out of the lead, until the finish line ends their anxiety. The last horse to be exposed in front is declared the winner and will never have to run in a Maiden race again.

People are not thoroughbreds and do not have the horse's instincts. The fastest runner is not necessarily the most respected person. Respect is not a function of speed afoot. The analogy can be instructive, however, because one way to achieve success involves being visible, standing out in front.

In ancient warfare, Greek hoplites would line up shoulder to shoulder with their shields forming a wall. To be part of this phalanx would be relatively safe. You shared protection and no one was trying to kill you specifically. To go out in front of the line, however, was dangerous. The enemy would target the lone figure. He did not have the protection of his neighbor's shield. He really was in greater danger. That was where the leader was expected to stand. That is why we call those in charge "leaders" and those they direct "followers.

Homer described a conversation between two warriors about to lead their soldiers into battle. The first, Glaukos, suggested that perhaps they would be better off staying hidden in the ranks. His companion, Sarpedon said something like this in reply. "If we could live forever, I would be out of here in a heartbeat. But we surely will die some day, so let us consider how we live. At the banquet, our wine cups are kept full. We get the best cuts of meat. We are honored and respected. It's great, but there is a price. We are treated like kings and in return we are expected to go out in front in battle."

In many circumstances of modern life, as well, there are great rewards for those who stand up and are visible. The band plays *Hail to the Chief* for the President, not for his speechwriter or for his advisors. A constant theme, whether in horse racing, Greek warfare, or business, is that there are rewards given to those who go in front, who strive and compete. For us, one way to achieve success involves getting up in front of others and talking. The one who stands up and delivers the results is seen by the audience as the one who achieved the results.

You need to decide if you want to be like a racehorse who tries to win or one who likes the security of the pack. It is not a matter of morality. One is not inherently better than the other. But if you want the prize, you have to try to win. The decision to strive to win does not assure victory; the competition has a say in the matter. Some very fine horses with clear instinctive drives to win found themselves in the same race as Secretariat and finished far behind. But you can decide to do the sorts of things that allow you to compete to the best of your ability.

So you need to decide who you want to be.

Don't be afraid that you cannot be who you want to be. The necessary steps will come in time.

The first time a journal editor asked me to recommend whether a submission should be published, my first thought was, "I have no idea if this is any good!" My second thought, however, was, "Of course I don't. That's because I haven't read it yet." I needed to slow down and take things one step at a time. First you read it, then you have an opinion. First you prepare your talk, then you are ready to give it.

Once I had read that paper, I had an opinion.

When deciding to become a speaker or when preparing to give a talk, do not fall into the trap of thinking, " But I'm not ready!" Of course you're not ready. It's not yet time to give it. But you will be, when the time comes, if you do the work.

If you have decided that you want to learn to make talking natural again, if you want to be a leader rather than a member of the crowd, you are ready to move on to how to do it.

Chapter Three

Success in Any Endeavor

When I was young, my friends and I would occasionally try to play tennis. We barely knew the rules and we definitely did not know how to hit a tennis ball. We whacked the ball as if we were hitting a baseball one-handed. The only way we could keep from hitting every shot long was to hit it softly. Only years later did I learn the mystery of topspin. Needless to say, we were incompetent tennis players and gave up the game until years later. We lacked the knowledge to play the game. Without that knowledge, we could not get started.

As a teenager, my friends and I began to try our hands at golf. A classmate, who caddied at a local course, gave me beginner's instructions. He showed me how to grip a club, to keep my left arm rigid and my right upper arm close to my body, and all the other basic technical skills necessary to play the game. I achieved moderate success because I had a certain level of knowledge to combine with general co-ordination. It had a limit, though, and I soon reached a plateau.

One day, I was playing eighteen holes with another friend. He watched me hit and after a while, as I was about to attempt a short iron to the green, he asked me what I was doing. I replied that I was holding my left arm straight, my right upper arm in, and so on. "That's the problem," he said. "You're playing mechanically. It's like you're a robot. That's no good.

"You're an athlete. Now that you know that other stuff, put it aside. Think about what you're trying to do – put the ball near the pin. Visualize it; let your body do what you want it to do. When you shoot a basketball, you don't think about where to put your arms or what angle the ball should travel. You just shoot for the hoop."

It clicked. My game made the largest improvement ever. Thinking of myself as an athlete allowed me to play like one. I had my identity straight and could do my best. I needed to know how to grip the club and all the rest, but knowing who I was let me do it well.

Twin pillars of knowledge are required for of success in any endeavor.[1] They are the practical knowledge of content and techniques and the knowledge of your identity or role. Both are integral to achieving the best possible results. Without technical knowledge you do not have the basics to do anything and without the proper sense of self you cannot do it well.

If a person with no training in ballet were to try to dance *en Pointe*, she would not be able. Knowledge of basic technique would be lacking. Similarly, if a talented dancer were to take the performance stage without knowing the music or the choreography, she would not be able to perform properly no matter how strong her technical ability or how good her mindset. Without the necessary knowledge of technique and of content, you do not have the ability even to get started. That basic level of knowledge is required to allow you at least to go through the basics of dancing, but it does not get you dancing well.

We might think of that sort of knowledge as the foundation of any endeavor. You cannot build on nothing. Without a strong foundation, a lasting structure cannot be built.[2] But on the other hand, foundations do not make very comfortable dwellings. Who wants to live in an unfinished concrete basement? So we need to build upon that foundation.

If our ballerina had mastered the basics of her craft, had learned the music and the choreography of a piece, and had practiced, she might well be capable of an adequate performance, but that would not be enough to make the dance come alive. Suppose she were to go onstage thinking "I hope I don't trip. I'll bet I do. I always mess up that *pas de deux*. I don't really feel like doing this today. God, I hate the stupid *Nutcracker*. Are we done yet?" With that sort of attitude, no one should expect her to give an inspired performance.

For many years, runners *knew* that it was impossible to run a mile in less than four minutes. It was like the sound barrier (also since broken) and the speed of light (which seems pretty solid.) But a student at Oxford University (a school more noted for scholarship than athletics) named Roger Bannister knew he that he indeed could do it and ran with that goal in mind. Once he had broken the four-minute mile, a number of other runners soon did likewise. Until Bannister did it, they ran "knowing" there was a limit to what they could achieve. Once they knew a mile could be run that fast, they could do it also.

Note that an overweight, out-of-shape, middle-aged smoker still could not run a 3'59" mile (or, perhaps even run a mile in any time limit.) One needed to be an elite runner for the altered mindset to have an effect. But the person with the physical tools to run that fast need to believe, even know (as Bannister did) that it could be done for it to become possible.

In the movie *The Empire Strikes Back*, Luke Skywalker had sunk his spaceship in a swamp. Yoda told him to use the Force to get it out of the water and as Luke began to try, the ship indeed levitated. Seeing his own success so startled Luke that he "dropped" the ship back into the swamp. Yoda then successfully lifted the ship and put it on dry land. Seeing this, Luke said he could not believe what he had just seen. Yoda replied that this disbelief was what kept Luke from doing it.

To be a successful presenter, you first must know what you are talking about. That means possessing the knowledge base you are trying to share. You cannot talk about subjects of which you know nothing. (There are those who can talk of subjects of which they are ignorant, but the names for people like that tend to include rude words.)

However, people frequently fail to speak well because they focus on the limits of their knowledge and lose sight of how much they know. They have not learned the technique of presenting what they do know rather than what they do not.

Equally important, you must know how to organize and deliver the message. You must know the techniques to make your information accessible to the audience. This includes having a sense of who the audience is as well as what you are trying to tell them.

That knowledge by itself can allow you to deliver a wooden, robotic talk or a panicky, anxiety-ridden one. In order to give a vibrant, lively, and comfortable one, you need to know your role and you need the correct attitude.[3] This is the characteristic of a great presenter.

In the following chapters you will learn how to organize your message and how to deliver it. We will begin with the first pillar, knowledge of the content the organization of that content. Next we will proceed to knowledge of your identity and role. Finally, we will put it all together and make talking natural again.

Chapter Four

What Do You Know?

Now that you are ready to learn to speak comfortably and clearly, the next step is to consider the content. What is the subject of your talk? What is the topic?

Two key elements need to be addressed before you open your mouth to begin any talk. The first is what you know; the second is what you want to say about it. These are not exactly the same thing, and so they will be addressed separately. Failure to differentiate between them is the on-ramp for the road to many a boring presentation. It seems like an obvious pair of steps, but many people stumble out of the starting gate because they fail to address these preliminaries.

First we will consider the issues and traps concerning what you do and do not know. In the following chapters we will proceed to selecting what to say from that pool of knowledge. Going through these preliminary steps before beginning to talk results in vastly improved communication. Ultimately, the attainable goal is to do this very quickly, effortlessly, and instinctively.

What is your knowledge base?

On any subject you can name, there are things you know and there are limits to your knowledge, things you do not know. Even when you would seem to have absolutely no knowledge of a subject, you at least know that single fact. If you were asked to speak about such a topic, the text would simply be "I don't know."

Usually, though, you do know something. Your knowledge may be vague and sketchy or it may be vast and deep, but you do know something. And unless the topic is a trivial one, there are details about the subject that you do not know. In fact, for any normally complex subject matter, there will always be vast amounts of information that you do not know. That is the nature of knowledge. Even the simplest bit of knowledge is part of a larger field, which is, in turn, part of a still larger universe of information.

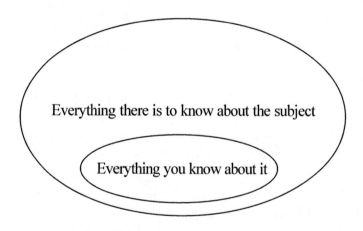

The diagram illustrates this point. The outer oval is a map of everything there is to know about any given subject, including what you know. The inner oval represents all that you know. Mathematicians would describe what you know as a sub-set of all there is to know. The overlap may be great or small as you know more or less of the subject, but they are never the same oval because you never know everything. For any interesting subject, this is *always* true.

But some may protest that it is certainly possible to know everything if you just study hard enough. They think it is simply a matter of effort. They are wrong.

Let's use your life as an example. You know a lot about yourself, more than you know about anything else. (This has to be true, because everything else you know is a part of your life.) You know your name. That bit of information is easy to know. (Sometimes it is not so easy to say it, as we will discuss later, but knowing it is simple.) More details of your life are also readily available. You can easily supply all sorts of stories and data about yourself. Eventually, though, you will get to information which is more difficult, or even impossible, to tell others because you do not know it. Do you remember who sat next to you in second grade? What did you dream last Thursday? What did you have for dinner on September 19, 1996? When did you learn to walk? What was the first movie you ever saw? What was the last movie you saw? And we are not even getting into questions like what are your pulse and respiration rate right now. Even if you knew the answers to all these specific questions, there are certainly some others that you could not answer. And this is about your life. You were there for all of it, so you know more about it than anyone else does. Even so, there are things you do not know.

You can never know everything.

But not everyone realizes this. Many people get caught in the trap of "I must know it all." They think they need to know everything, as if it were possible to know everything. They feel that unless they know every detail and are ready to answer every possible question, they are unprepared to speak. As a result, these people are never ready to give a talk. Sometimes they fool themselves into feeling "totally ready." They go out to talk full of false confidence, thinking they know everything. Sometimes they are not confronted with their limits, and they can hold on to the illusion of omniscience. When this happens, it reinforces their mistaken belief system. "I knew everything and it was okay." At other times, however, they are startled by an unexpected question. When that happens, their confidence is shaken. They feel they went out unprepared, and that if they had just been a little more thorough in their preparation, they would have been ready for anything. Next time, they vow, they will be thoroughly prepared. They keep thinking that they can know everything, if only they prepare well enough.

A reporter once asked Michael Jordan how long his tongue was. Who could possibly anticipate a question like that? You can never know everything about your topic.

Some other people make the mistake of "I don't know it all, so I don't know anything." They are aware of the limits of their knowledge. In fact, they are so aware of what they do not know that they forget that they do know something. When asked to talk, they think about all the things outside of the limits of their knowledge and are overwhelmed. When asked a question, unless the answer immediately pops into mind, they are paralyzed and unable to think of what they do know. They look at what is outside of the inner oval rather than what is inside it. Imagine someone asked to describe life on earth and thinking instead of the lack of life in outer space.

Consider an analyst at a brokerage firm who is discussing a certain company, XYZ Corp. Someone might ask the price of the stock at that moment. While this is a generally reasonable question, if it were the middle of the trading day the analyst could not know the exact answer unless the ticker was in view, an unlikely scenario. The analyst could seize the exact question and, aware of what he does not know, acknowledge ignorance. Or he could instead focus on what was within his field of knowledge. "They closed at 58 yesterday were up to 59 when I checked just before coming in. Trading was moderate, so they should be around that price." He focused on what he did know, not on what he did not.

There are two points to remember. You always know something. You never know everything. You can only talk about what you know, and you can talk all about what you know.

Now let's look inside that area of knowledge that you actually have.

Chapter Five

Presenting Vertically

We have established that you have a great amount of information you could share with your audience. You could drift along all day, perhaps, vaguely moving from thought to thought, and unless your listeners are really into rambling, the talk will be a failure. What exactly do you know? How can you make sense of your knowledge in order to be able to share it?

To answer that question, we need to go back to what you know and put it into some order. Once we have, the process to organize your talk will become clear. You are about to learn the vertical organization of any talk. You will learn to see your talk as a triangle with a precise tip and as large a base as needs be. Everything in the triangle will connect vertically, from top to bottom.

Frequently, people have tons of information about a given subject. In fact, often they have so much that they have no real understanding of just what knowledge they do have. Data is floating around in their brains in great quantity, but finding a specific bit can be difficult or impossible. This can result in a disorganized stream of words that are incomprehensible to listeners and frustrate both speaker and audience.

During World War II, the United States formed the OSS, the precursor of the CIA, to figure out what the Nazis were going to do.

Among the first people they recruited were librarians. The OSS leadership knew that soon they would be swamped with bits of information from various sources and they would need to organize it if it were to be of any real use. Librarians were accustomed to taking huge amounts of data and making it accessible through organization. In modern technology, this is what data mining programs do.

Imagine thousands, or even millions of index cards, each with a single bit of information on it. (Sounds like a lot of people's brains, with brain cells for index cards.) Imagine them spread out all over the floor. There would be lots of information, but no way to use it effectively. To use it would require order.

One familiar way to organize information is by categorizing and grouping data. Basic ideas are put with similar ones and form categories, which then are formed into super-categories, and so forth. Think of taking those index cards and clustering those that shared some common trait.

As a simple illustration, imagine a deck of playing cards. (It may help if instead you go get a deck of cards and actually do this exercise.) You begin with 52 bits of information, the individual cards. You might decide to put together cards with the same value and color, so red threes, black kings, red aces, etc. form pairs. (Remember, you are determining how to group them. There is not some Aristotelian Absolute way of ordering them. It is your structure. You decide how they fit together.) At the end of this sorting you would have gone from 52 individual cards to 26 pairs. Take these resultant pairs of cards and organize them, putting all the red face cards in one group, the red number cards in another, and so on with the blacks. Next, put all the reds together and the blacks in the other category. Finally, put them together as a single deck of cards.

You can arrive at this particular organization via the opposite direction, as well. Begin with a single category in mind, a deck of cards, and break it into the sub-categories into which items are assigned. First you put the Reds on one side and the Blacks on the other. Next, separate the face cards from the number cards, so you have four piles of cards, two on each side of the table. Now you pair each card with another of the same value and color (e.g. Ace of Spades with Ace of Clubs, Three of hearts with Three of Diamonds, etc.). You could continue the process in as fine a detail as one wished. (You could rip up the cards to make more than 52 basic bits of data.)

You can visualize this sort of organization as a triangle, whose tip is the essence of the category (in this case, a deck of cards) and whose base is the raw data (the 52 cards) with progressively larger groupings in the middle. As just described, you can achieve this triangle by starting at either the top or the bottom. The end result is the same. However you get there, you end up with 52 cards, 26 pairs, four groups, two colors, and a single deck.

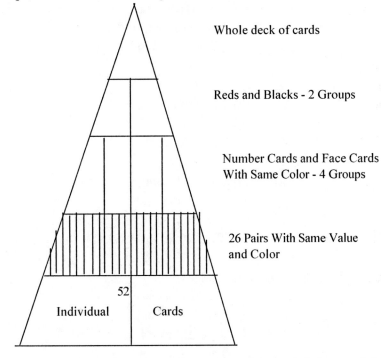

Whole deck of cards

Reds and Blacks - 2 Groups

Number Cards and Face Cards With Same Color - 4 Groups

26 Pairs With Same Value and Color

52 Individual Cards

Each layer contains all the information of the ones below and the ones above. The deck contains all the cards and all their groupings. Reds is contained in Deck and contains Red Numbers or Faces, Red Pairs, and Red Cards. A Red Pair is part of all the larger Red Groups and contains two Red Cards. As you move down or up, the level of detail increases or decreases, but the essential elements remain the same. Everything within this triangle relates vertically to its sub-categories and super-categories. Everything about those cards is part of the Deck.

This is not a foreign concept. Most people learn to make an outline in grammar school with a theme and pieces organized below as follows:

Theme of the Outline

I. First Major Point

    A. First Point Under I.
        1. First Point Under A.
            a. First Point Under 1.
            b. Second Point Under 1.
            c. Third Point Under 1.

        2. Second Point Under A
            a. First Point Under 2.
            b. Second Point Under 2.
            c. Third Point Under 2.

        3. Third Point Under A.
            a. First Point Under 3.
            b. Second Point Under 3
            c. Third Point Under 3.

    B. Second Point Under I.
        1. First Point Under B.
            a. First Point Under 1.
            b. Second Point Under 1.
            c. Third Point Under 1.

        2. Second Point Under B.
            a. First Point Under 2.
            b. Second Point Under 2.
            c. Third Point Under 2.

        3. Third Point Under B.
            a. First Point Under 3.
            b. Second Point Under 3
            c. Third Point Under 3.

C. Third Point Under I.
    1. First Point Under C.
        a. First Point Under 1.
        b. Second Point Under 1.
        c. Third Point Under 1.

    2. Second Point Under C.
        a. First Point Under 2.
        b. Second Point Under 2.
        c. Third Point Under 2.

    3. Third Point Under C.
        a. First Point Under 3.
        b. Second Point Under 3
        c. Third Point Under 3.

II. Second Major Point

A. First Point Under II.
    1. First Point Under A.
        a. First Point Under 1.
        b. Second Point Under 1.
        c. Third Point Under 1.

    2. Second Point Under A
        a. First Point Under 2.
        b. Second Point Under 2.
        c. Third Point Under 2.

    3. Third Point Under A.
        a. First Point Under 3.
        b. Second Point Under 3
        c. Third Point Under 3.

B. Second Point Under II.
    1. First Point Under B.
        a. First Point Under 1.
        b. Second Point Under 1.

       c.   Third Point Under 1.

   2.   Second Point Under B.
       a.   First Point Under 2.
       b.   Second Point Under 2.
       c.   Third Point Under 2.

   3.   Third Point Under B.
       a.   First Point Under 3.
       b.   Second Point Under 3
       c.   Third Point Under 3.

III. Third Major Point

  A.   First Point Under III.
     1.   First Point Under A.
       a.   First Point Under 1.
       b.   Second Point Under 1.
       c.   Third Point Under 1.

     2.   Second Point Under A
       a.   First Point Under 2.
       b.   Second Point Under 2.
       c.   Third Point Under 2.

     3.   Third Point Under A.
       a.   First Point Under 3.
       b.   Second Point Under 3
       c.   Third Point Under 3.
  B.   First Point Under III.
     1.   First Point Under B.
       a.   First Point Under 1.
       b.   Second Point Under 1.
       c.   Third Point Under 1.

     2.   Second Point Under B.
       a.   First Point Under 2.

     b. Second Point Under 2.

     c. Third Point Under 2.

3.   Third Point Under B.

     a. First Point Under 3.

     b. Second Point Under 3

     c. Third Point Under 3.

This triangle turns the outline on its side to make a visual map to aid organization of topics.

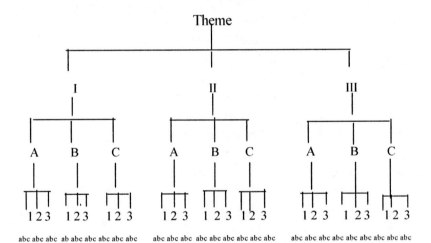

Let's take a minute to outline our deck of cards in the classic fashion, showing how you can turn a triangle into an outline and vice versa.

A Deck of Cards

I. Black Cards

   A. Black Number Cards

      1. Pairs of Black Aces

         a. Ace of Clubs

         b. Ace of Spades

2. Pairs of Black Twos
    a. Two of Clubs
    b. Two of Spades
3. Pairs of Black Threes
    a. Three of Clubs
    b. Three of Spades
4. Pairs of Black Fours
    a. Four of Clubs
    b. Four of Spades
5. Pair of Black Fives
    a. Five of Clubs
    b. Five of Spades
6. Pair of Black Sixes
    a. Six of Clubs
    b. Six of Spades
7. Pair of Black Sevens
    a. Seven of Clubs
    b. Seven of Spades
8. Pair of Black Eights
    a. Eight of Clubs
    b. Eight of Spades
9. Pair of Black Nines
    a. Nine of Clubs
    b. Nine of Spades
10. Pair of Black Tens
    a. Ten of Clubs
    b. Ten of Spades

B. Black Face Cards
1. Pair of Black Jacks
    a. Jack of Clubs
    b. Jack of Spades
2. Pair of Black Queens
    a. Queen of Clubs
    b. Queen of Spades
3. Pair of Black Kings
    a. King of Clubs
    b. King of Spades

II. Red Cards
  A. Red Number Cards
      1. Pairs of Red Aces
            a. Ace of Diamonds
            b. Ace of Hearts
      2. Pairs of Red Twos
            a. Two of Clubs
            b. Two of Hearts
      3. Pairs of Black Threes
            a. Three of Diamonds
            b. Three of Hearts
      4. Pairs of Red Fours
            a. Four of Clubs
            b. Four of Hearts
      5. Pair of Black Fives
            a. Five of Diamonds
            b. Five of Hearts
      6. Pair of Red Sixes
            a. Six of Diamonds
            b. Six of Hearts
      7. Pair of Black Sevens
            a. Seven of Diamonds
            b. Seven of Hearts
      8. Pair of Red Eights
            a. Eight of Diamonds
            b. Eight of Hearts
      9. Pair of Red Nines
            a. Nine of Diamonds
            b. Nine of Hearts
      10. Pair of Black Tens
            a. Ten of Diamonds
            b. Ten of Hearts

  B. Red Face Cards
      1. Pair of Black Jacks
            a. Jack of Diamonds
            b. Jack of Hearts

2. Pair of Red Queens
    a. Queen of Diamonds
    b. Queen of Hearts
3. Pair of Black Kings
    a. King of Diamonds
    b. King of Hearts

Notice the mastery over the data you obtain by this structure. You not only know what you know, you also know where every fact is and how it relates to every other bit of information. Contrast the ease of finding a given card, say the Six of Clubs, in this paradigm (It has to be under I. [Black], A. [Number Cards], 6 [Sixes] and there it is at I.A.6.a.) with picking up a shuffled deck (which may or may not contain all fifty-two cards) and hunting through it to find a certain card which may or may not be there. But a fifty-two-bit database is easy to handle even in the absence of structure. The importance of organization is proportional to the complexity and size of the topic.

Think of what this does to your ability to handle questions. You know how to find answers. You not only know the information, you know where to find it.

We can apply this organizational strategy to more than a just a simple deck of cards. A complex example from real life can help to illustrate that this vertical concept can handle the largest cases.

Think of the classic Linnaean Organization of Living Things. The summation or tip of this triangle is Life. Beneath are the five Kingdoms of simple cells, large celled life, molds and fungi, plants, and animals.

These categories can then be broken into sub-groups as illustrated below:

Sean F. Kelly and Reid J. Kelly

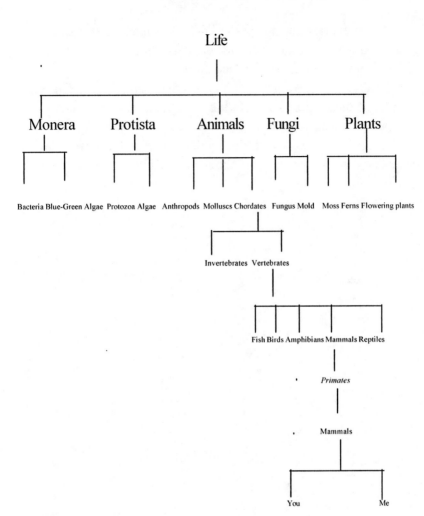

The categories are not pre-ordained. It may be instructive to consider organizing a familiar structure into this sort of format in two different ways. Let us consider the train.

A train is a single entity, but it is also made up of parts. One way to think of these parts is by looking at large pieces, such as engines and cars. Cars can be classified by type, such as passenger car and freight car. These can be sub-divided into sleeping car, coach, dining car, cattle car, tank car, and container car. The hierarchy would look like this:

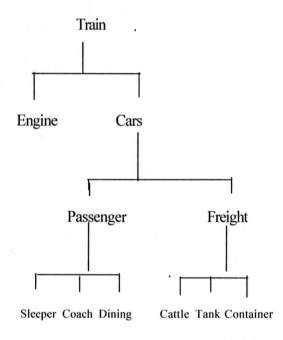

Train

Engine   Cars

Passenger   Freight

Sleeper Coach Dining   Cattle Tank Container

But this is not the only way to organize a train. One could instead pay attention to the components that make up all the larger pieces as follows:

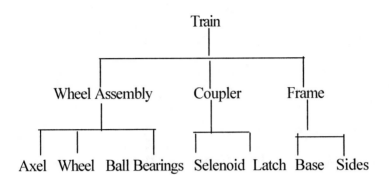

Understand that the choice of how to organize the pieces, or even what pieces to consider, is not imposed from without, but rather is a choice made by the organizer.

Note also that all of these organizations are simultaneously made up of smaller sub-groups that could stand alone (e.g. Mammals or Passenger Cars) while they are also part of larger. Life is a sub-set of All Things on the Planet, Living and Non-living. Trains are a part of the category of Transportation along with Planes, Trucks, and Boats.

In theory, then, you know how to organize and arrange everything you know about a subject. You rarely, or more likely never, will put all of your thoughts on a subject into order, but you could. More specifically, you would know how to find a place for any idea or fact that came along, just as biologists know how to place a new species in the Linnaean Organization and librarians know how to determine where to shelve a just-written book.

Bit now you want to apply this to giving a talk.

Chapter Six

The Point of Your Talk

Now you have your knowledge organized so it is accessible in a logical sort of a way. You see how parts fit together and what the hierarchy of ideas is. You have a handle on what you have.

Now the next question arises. What do you want to say? What exactly is your message?

When you choose to give a talk, you must decide what you want to tell the audience. Almost everyone thinks they do this already. They know what they are talking about. Kind of. More or less. When pushed to be really specific about their theme, however, they frequently discover that their focus is vague and fuzzy. In other words, they do not really know.

If the focus is vague and fuzzy, the talk will be as well.

Unless you are just chatting aimlessly, you should always be trying to make a point. If you do not have a coherent, unified theme, your communication will be unclear. If you do not know what that point is, how can your audience? How could you make something if you do not know what it is? You cannot.

Now this point is not necessarily something you will say aloud or acknowledge. It might be implicit or even subliminal, but it needs to be clear in your mind. It needs to be there as THE point of reference in your mind.

If someone asked an attentive member of the audience what you had said, you were clear if he or she could reply in a concise sentence. Elaborations could follow, but the theme would be known. You need to know in advance what that answer would be.

In a single simple sentence, state the one theme of your talk. It could less than a sentence, just a phrase, or even a word, but it must be no more than a short, simple sentence.

If you do not know what that sentence is, you do not know what message you are trying to deliver. People often think they know a subject clearly until they try to reduce it to its basics. When Noble Prize-winning physicist Richard Feynman found himself unable to explain in a single lecture why spin ½ particles obey Fermi-Dirac statistics (whatever that means) to Cal Tech freshmen, he concluded, "That means we really don't understand it." [4] Feynman clearly knew lots about those particles, so much that everyone thought he could explain them. It was when he attempted to extract the essence of that understanding that he discovered the gaps in his knowledge. Even the most complex topics must be reduced to manageable size if the audience is to understand the message. That means going through the advance work of really understanding what you want to say.

This problem is often seen in the case of people who know how to do something quite well, but who have not consciously organized the process. A common example can be seen in travel. Many times, a person can drive from one place to another effortlessly, but when asked to give verbal directions cannot do so. They cannot put what they know into words.

Once you have your theme sentence, the work is not done. Now you need to add the main sub-themes, the major pieces. Think of building a skeleton for your talk. You eventually need to flesh out the body of the talk, but first you need the bones. Your theme is the backbone, and now you are adding the arms and legs. Eventually the fingers and toes will be added. As described in the triangles within triangles image, you are constructing a talk consisting of pieces, each of which has a key point. Each sub-triangle has a point to make, and everything within it must relate to that point.

This succinctness of topic does not have to mean that the talk is brief. The ideas you are expressing may be lengthy and complex, but they all need to connect with your theme and you need to know how the connection is made.

Let's go back to Linnaeus and his catalogue. That certainly has the capacity to serve as the basis of an extremely long and complex lecture, or more properly, set of lectures. The content would be every creature that has ever lived! A more massive topic would be hard to imagine. But what would be the theme? It would be a single word. Life.

Everything that Linnaeus could say would be related to that topic. Whatever living creature he might discuss would be connected to his theme. Not only would it be related to his theme, he could trace in his mind how it was related. He would have an underlying sense of order that would keep him from wandering hopelessly from one creature to the next. The pieces, living creatures, fit into a pattern, a logical matrix, which has the power to keep the talk comprehensible. There is a clear vertical pathway connecting every creature to Life and Life to every creature.

This organization of information is a crucial process in the delivery of a talk. Before you begin to talk, you need to decide what your message is. Everything you say must relate to that theme. If you have an idea it must have a clear (to you) connection to your theme, to the tip of your hierarchy. If something does not connect to the theme sentence, that you must leave it out, no matter how interesting and informative, or else you must change or adjust your theme topic.

You do not have to explicitly tell your audience what your theme is, but you have to know it yourself. If you do, there will be an underlying clarity of purpose that will make it easier for your audience to follow along. Even if they are not consciously aware of it, they will find it easier to follow because it all fits together. Patterns are comprehended where random behavior is not.

There are two benefits to having this vertical organization sharp and clear in your mind. First, the audience will more easily comprehend and follow you. Second, you will have confidence because you will have a manageable task to perform.

This book is a written communication. But it could be (and, in fact, has been) presented in a spoken format. Everything in this book relates to a simple theme: Talking is natural. Every word relates to that common purpose. The discussion of the difficulties people encounter, or create for themselves, is an elaboration of that theme.

Underneath that main theme are four topics: Making the decision to talk, Technical knowledge of the content, Knowledge of your role or identity, and Technical issues. The first of these has been covered. So far, the second has been broken into the following pieces: Defining what you know, Organizing that knowledge, and Presenting vertically. The talk/book continues to grow, covering more of Content, and then moving through the remaining topics. Throughout, there will be an organization that should facilitate your learning and serve as a pattern for your understanding.

When you begin to formulate a talk, once you have your main topic, you must then decide what points you wish to make about that theme. Next, go on and decide what points will be useful to support those bits, and so on. Your talk is almost ready to write itself, but first we must consider super-points and presenting horizontally.

Chapter Seven

The Super-Point of Your Talk

Not infrequently, there is actually what I would call a super-point to a talk, the most important, but not explicitly mentioned, reason for the talk. Lack of awareness of this super-point can blunt the effectiveness of the best speaker. The idea can be transmitted without the why of it. Some examples of super-points may illuminate the concept.

Imagine the executive team of a growing corporation going to talk to investment bankers or venture capitalists seeking capital for expansion. They will go with their PowerPoint deck and business model and financials to describe the investment and try to persuade the bankers to join. They would make a serious tactical error if they behaved as if this were an academic b-school exercise. Throughout their pitch, the super-point has to be "We can both make a lot of money doing this." All of their talk *per se* is about the details, how that money can be made, but the super-point is to motivate them to buy into the plan.

An investment brokerage firm hosted a symposium for large investors. During the day, CEOs from major manufacturing corporations gave presentations on their view of their relationship with America's trading partners. A senior partner from the brokerage firm was to welcome each CEO and act as emcee. He thought his task was simply to introduce each executive and keep the proceedings flowing smoothly. He was wrong. His super-point was to show the investors that he was well known by the CEOs and, therefore, that he (and his firm) could deliver the best, most well informed information about this sector of the economy and so should be their brokerage firm. His super-point was "We can give you the insights you need."

An associate in a law firm reports to a partner on the progress she has made in negotiating an acquisition for a client. The official point of the meeting is to update the partner on the status of the deal. The super-point is "I am an asset to this firm."

A CEO gave an annual state of the company address to the investors who owned his company and reported very successful results in an extremely understated fashion. The effect was that the investors were left with a strong impression that the firm lacked leadership at the top. He needed to realize that the super-point of his presentation was not merely that the company's numbers were good but also that the leadership team was strong and competent, deserving of credit and faith. His personal modesty prevented him from taking an appropriately celebratory stance. When given the image of the US Ryder Cup team celebrating their victory openly, in contrast to their placid demeanor in the face of success on the PGA tour, he was able to show more pride in accomplishment.

A politician on the campaign trail speaks about his policy positions. His super-point is "Vote for me." He does not want the voters to elect another candidate to implement his ideas. He wants to do it. (A cynic might say that some politicians do not care what policies are implemented as long as they are the ones in office. There the super-point is the only real point.)

Know not only what point you are trying to get across but also why you are doing this in the first place.

Chapter Eight

Presenting Horizontally
Part One: The Destination

Once you have figured out the point (and super-point) of what you want to say, after you have the vertical elements sharp and clear in your mind, it is time to plan the horizontal elements of your talk.

Vertical organization makes you understand how your thoughts and ideas fit together. Horizontal organization is how you plan to deliver these organized ideas to the audience. Of course there is much communality between the two. Both are preparing for the same talk. If there were not a lot of overlap you would have a very schizophrenic talk. You are talking about your vertically arranged ideas. But planning the transmission of these ideas to others requires a slightly different approach, a horizontal view.

Think of a presentation as a journey of the mind. The speaker is a guide, leading the audience to a chosen destination. When you are presenting, whether formally or informally, you are taking your listeners with you on this journey, and the more clearly you lead them, the better able they will be to follow.

The Internet has introduced us to a variety of high-tech means of finding our way through the world; several on-line services provide maps and directions. All of them, however, have a structure and process that is unchanged since asking directions from time immemorial. If you want directions, you need to provide two initial bits of information. Where do you want to go? Where is your starting point? Once those two questions are answered, the third step, picking out points along the way that mark the path from origin to destination, is easy.

Note that in physical reality and in the world of presenting there is more than one way to get from here to there. Some pathways are more direct, some more scenic, and some are just more familiar. All can be used to arrive at the same place, though not the same time. Choosing the origin and end-point do not dictate the route between.

The horizontal organization of your talk is the plan or road map for bringing your audience from where they are to where you want them to be. As in any mapping out of a route, there are three points to cover and a specific, and not necessarily obvious, order in developing them. First comes the destination, where you want the audience to end up, then comes the starting point, where they are when you meet them, and then, finally, the points along the way from start to finish. The reason for tackling them in this sequence is that unless you know the destination, you do not know what elements of the starting point are most relevant. In the physical world, a nearby airport is irrelevant if planning a trip downtown, and the presence of a subway stop is beside the point for a Sunday drive. And until you know the start and finish, you cannot begin to plan the trip.

So first of all we will consider the destination.

Just as in the real physical world of travel, there are different sorts of destinations. If I want to go to the southwest corner of the observation deck of the Empire State Building, the end-point is quite specific. If I want to find a Hunan restaurant in San Francisco, there are multiple destinations that meet the criteria within a fairly small geographic area. As a guide I could choose one and take the audience there, I could ask them for more information to help decide on one, or I could merely take them to Chinatown and let them go from there on their own.

Sometimes the destination cannot be specified precisely in advance, but rather is defined by some clear but imprecise parameters. When

President Thomas Jefferson sent Lewis and Clark on their expedition, he did not say, "Go to Seattle." They were told to go west, looking for a Northwest Passage, until they came to the end of the continent. They knew they had not arrived when they were crossing the Rockies and they knew they had reached their goal when they got to the Pacific Ocean. The goal was not vague, they just did not know exactly where it was.

Where you want to bring your listeners is closely related to the point of your talk, but it is not exactly identical to it. The subtle difference is that the point of your talk is the overarching idea that shapes the content of your ideas. The destination is what you want to achieve as a result of the talk. It is your goal for the audience.

The destination may be a state of knowledge or information about a subject. In a calculus lecture, for example, the professor's aim is to have the students understand integrals and functions. There is no debate about it; there are mathematics for the student to learn. Or the destination may be to understand a position, possibly controversial, without a judgment on the part of the listeners. In the classroom next door, an Economics professor may be describing competing theories of macroeconomics. The goal is to inform the students of the differing views, but not to convince them of the superiority of one over the other. In both classes, the instructor's point is the content of the material; the goal is the passage of knowledge or information to the students.

Frequently, the destination is persuasion of the audience, to get a decision by the listeners to do what you want them to do. You are telling them about a reorganization proposal, for example, in order to get them to agree to implement it. You are explaining your position so others will see the merits of your position. You are pleading before a jury in order to get the desired verdict. Selling is a particular version of this type of destination. You want the listener to buy or to invest.[5] The point of your pitch is the content of the material, the destination is the desired action taken on that knowledge.

A hybrid of the informative and persuasive presentation would be one where action is the goal but the speaker is disinterested in the outcome. A portfolio manager could describe two competing investment strategies to an investor, describing the merits and risks of each. She wants her client to be able to choose wisely based on the best information, but her commission and fees will be unaffected by which decision is made. The point is the understanding of the market; the destination is an investment decision, but not a particular one.

Another type of destination is related to the persuasive one. This one is intended to inspire the audience emotionally, to get them involved rather than simply intellectually agreeing. When Knute Rockne addressed the Fighting Irish in the locker room at half time and described George Gipp's deathbed, his closing entreaty, to "Win one for the Gipper!" was intended to inspire. The point of the talk was the memory of George Gipp. The destination was to put them in a state of desire, camaraderie, and motivation that would make them an unstoppable force on the gridiron

Sometimes the destination is to get the audience to give you information in order to allow you to move forward. An architect would present preliminary plans for a proposed building to get feed-back which would allow him to hone his vision to meet the client's vision. The point is the state of the design at this time, but the destination is client input as a guide for proceeding.

Sometimes the destination is to have gone through a presentation to fulfill external requirements. Human Relations representative spend part of their time giving annual talks on subjects like sexual harassment. No major corporation would ever go on record as promoting, condoning, or even turning a blind eye to sexual harassment in the workplace. Cynics might well doubt whether such a talk would have any significant effect anyway, because those who would behave improperly are not likely to be dissuaded by a lecture. Why bother? Because of liability. If the corporation can demonstrate that it has communicated a clear policy against sexual harassment, it would have a defense against a claim based upon an employee's misconduct. The point of the talk is to establish that corporate policy forbids sexual harassment. The goal of the talk is to be able to say to a court or an underwriter "We told them not to."

In all of these cases, the presenter has determined in advance why he or she is talking to these people, where they are supposed to end up. When you are preparing to speak, you need likewise to decide where you are taking your audience.

The world of high-level athletics can give an insight into how to maximize preparation by thinking of results. A major imaginal tool employed by world-class athletes is to visualize results before they happen. Successful field goal kickers, for example, deal with a time-out before they kick by mentally seeing the ball go through the uprights. Thinking of success is, in effect, to practice success, and that increases the odds of achieving it.

When preparing, think ahead in time to just after you speak. Think of yourself having just given an excellent talk. Listen to the terrific feedback you receive. Let yourself bask in the success you achieved. Like a field goal kicker, mentally planning for success or failure does much to determine which you achieve.

If you do not know where you are going, how will you know when, or whether, you have arrived?

Chapter Nine

Presenting Horizontally
Part Two: The Starting Point

Now you know where you want to bring your audience. But you cannot lead them there until you go get them. You need to figure out where they are, another seemingly obvious but frequently overlooked step in the process of a good presentation. Once you know where they are, you need to go there yourself. A guide has to go to where his charges are to begin the journey.

Understanding where they are involves assessing three audience elements. The first is their knowledge base, the second is their interest in listening, and the third is their emotional state, which includes their physical state.

It is important to note that picking out a starting point is not the same as having a good opening line. It is true that the opening words and sentences of a talk are absolutely vital to its success. This is a topic that is addressed in great detail later. While the opening lines are key to getting audience attention, they are not the more basic knowing where the audience is before you begin. The opening is an outgrowth of recognizing where the audience is. You cannot craft a good opening without knowing where the audience is, but where they are has to come before how you address them. Think of the opening statement as being like decoration. Before you decorate, you must have something substantive to paint.

Using this book as a model of a presentation (Remember, it has been delivered in spoken format.), you can see that I decided to target my remarks to a group of people who were interested in improving their ability to present in public. I thought that they would be people who were talented and knowledgeable and who were motivated to improve their skill set.

Go back to the first page and see that I thought I knew who that audience was. Once I had that, I could open with "Talking is natural." I knew whom I was addressing and how I wanted to connect with them.

Sometimes, the opening words are not obviously connected to knowing where the audience is. "Four score and seven years ago, our fathers brought forth on this continent a new nation, conceived in Liberty, and dedicated to the proposition that all men are created equal." Perhaps the greatest and certainly the best known opening lines in American oration, Lincoln did not state that he knew who his listeners were, but he clearly knew and so could immediately connect.

For now, we are going to stay with the first step, understanding where your audience is.

First of all, their knowledge state. If you talk too far over the heads of your listeners or talk down to them, you will lose them before you begin. In the opening lines of *The Iliad*, Homer jumps into the Trojan War nine and a half years into the story of a ten-year conflict. He knew his Greek listeners were familiar with the tale so there was no need to bring them up to speed. A book intended to tell the same story to modern readers would probably begin the narrative at the abduction of Helen or earlier.

It is important, then, to understand how much they know about what you want to say. Suppose you were to be given the task of describing a new computer system that was to be used to track the flow of inventory in your company. If you were speaking to the IT department, you would know that they both knew about and also cared about the technical details. They want to hear about operating systems and processors, gigabytes and gigahertz and GUIs. When talking to the people on the shipping dock, the starting point needs to be at applications. Which button do you press to show that you have shipped a part to an internal customer? And if you were talking to the executive officers of the company, they probably just want to know what impact the new system will have on profitability.

There is a special problem confronting you when your audience contains a mix of knowledgeable and naïve listeners. The issues of how to keep them interested is addressed later, but for now, you need to recognize that you have to find some shared meeting ground from whence to embark upon your journey.

The interest of the audience is the second factor to consider.

Sometimes it is the job of the listener to pay attention. If you are recommending action on a major financing application to the loan committee at the bank where you work, they will (or should be) giving you their attention because they will be responsible for the decision they make. An attorney should be able to assume the interest of the judge and jury when he or she is in court.

If you were meeting with newly hired employees on their first day of work to explain their benefits package to them, the attention would be mixed. They would want to learn about what they are getting, but also they might be feeling anxious and overwhelmed as well as eager to go to their new desks and actually get started.

The CEO of a heavy manufacturing company prepared a speech every year and went around to deliver it to everyone in the company. It was in many ways a fine speech, but it failed miserably because he gave it unchanged to very different groups. It was not that he needed to hide things from one or another group, but he failed to note where his audience was when he began. For example, when he spoke of reduced accidents on the floor of the plant, the workers were glad to hear that the risk of death or mutilation by spilled molten steel was less. This was a literal flesh and blood issue to them. The investors in the company and the board of directors, while caring people, saw the same issue primarily as one of reduced insurance premiums and workers comp costs, thus improving the bottom line.

Some talks, like that of the H.R. director reviewing sexual harassment policies, are really formalities, where the audience will pay little attention and all the speaker can hope to do with most of the audience is to have them go through the motions of listening. Think of the instructions of an airplane flight crew teaching you how to fasten your seat belt and explaining that oxygen is flowing even though the bag does not inflate.

The emotional state of the audience is sometimes important. Most of the time, it can correctly be assumed to be neutral. The investors want to hear the financials, the CEO wants an update, or the potential investor wants to hear about the opportunity. Sometimes, though, the emotional state demands attention.

A major event can grossly interfere with listening. For example, if it were announced that there would be a round of lay-offs tomorrow, people would not be ready to pay full attention to a description of long-range planning. Sometimes the best thing in that case is to put aside your planned remarks and let the audience spend some time talking about the short-term future, before you return to your planned issues.

If an audience is hostile, putting on your best Mr. Rogers' Neighborhood happy face is not likely to go far. That does not mean you need to go in ready for a fight (though that may be your best strategy), but it usually helps to acknowledge the obvious. If there is tension in the air, you need to know about it and begin accordingly.

A man was teaching his son to ride a bike and, as usually happens, the boy fell and landed on his face, getting a bloody nose. The father ran over and said, "That must hurt a lot. But at least your blood is nice and red. That means you are healthy. Let me get out my handkerchief so we can see how red it is against the white cloth."

The boy, who was not seriously hurt, got caught up in looking at his healthy blood, and was easily led into the bathroom, "where we can see the healthy red color against the porcelain." The key to this interaction was the opening acknowledgement "That must hurt a lot." If the father had tried to begin by distracting with a focus on red blood, his son would have kept saying, "No, you don't understand. It hurts." When the father started by acknowledging hurt, the son knew his father understood the pain and was ready to be distracted.

"The earnings for the past quarter are disappointing," confronts the reality and tells the listeners that you know they are not happy. Now you can go on to deliver the rest of the message.

Mental state can be predicted from the structure of events. If you are the last presenter at a conference and the attendees are all eager to catch flights home as soon as you are done, you need to take that into consideration.

Finally, consider the physical state.

If you are speaking at the end of a long day of speakers, or just after a heavy lunch, your audience is going to be tired or post-prandial. You will be battling drowsiness. If you have them first thing in the morning, it may take a while for them to get into gear. You may want to do something to energize them. Similarly, be aware of the effects of sitting for extended periods of time, particularly after multiple cups of coffee.

If you keep yourself aware of these, assessing where you are meeting the audience, you will be in good shape to lead them on the journey to the destination.

Next, how do you get there from here?

Chapter Ten

Presenting Horizontally
Part Three: The Path

You know the ends of the journey, now you need to connect them. This is the final step to preparing a presentation.

A straight line is not the only path between two points. There are many ways to get from here to there, and the choice of highway or scenic trail is yours to make. You can wander aimlessly until you hit the destination by chance, you can march directly, or you can proceed in a straightforward manner while allowing for side trips. The choice is yours. Like most things, however, it is preferable to choose actively rather than simply let it happen.

An important key to clear, persuasive presenting is to remember that the more clear and sharp the steps along the way, the easier it will be for your audience to follow (and so to agree with you) and the easier it will be for them to recall what you said.

People who have to memorize lists know that learning is easier if a pattern or order is established, something that transforms a bunch of random bits into a coherent whole. When asked to remember an assortment of objects on a table, mnemonists will imagine how all of them could be used is a sequence of tasks, or think of passing stores and seeing them in the windows of the shops. Devices such as taking the initial letters of the names of things and making a catchy phrase with those initials works well. The planets, in sequence from the sun, can be remembered by "Mary's Violet Eyes Make John Sit Up Now Promptly." Generations of medical students have learned the twelve cranial nerves with the bawdy "Oh, Oh, Oh, To Touch And Feel…"

The more logical and orderly the progression of ideas, the more the listener can readily follow you, the more effective you will be. This does not mean that the structure needs to be spelled out overtly, only that it has to be present.

One excellent way to connect start and finish is to plan a series of points connecting the two. They need not be numerous; in fact, you should think of a few keys and no more. There is no fixed number of points along the way. The number depends on what you have to say. However, it should be a fairly small number. The plan can be visualized as below:

Where the Audience Is

     First Point

        Second Point

           Third Point

              Fourth Point

                 Where You Are going

For talks that recur, you can even develop a template for all such talks. For example, a commercial credit officer pitching a possible deal to her loan committee would typically have the following points to present: 1) Basic data; 2) Problems and concerns; 3) Mitigants; 4) Recommendation of action. And, obviously, the beginning is that the loan committee wants to hear about proposed business and the final point is reaching the decision to make the loan (the officer hopes.)

Looking at this example, it is clear that each point along the way, while summarized by its title, requires elaboration. Basic data needs expansion to give the company name, its history with the bank, the type of loan requested, the amount, the collateral, and the terms. The problems and possible factors that would lead to refusal of credit need to be spelled out, as do the mitigating factors. All of these need more detail.

This should remind you of something. We are back to vertical organization and points of triangles. Each point of the horizontal presentation schematic is the tip or theme statement of a vertically arranged set of thoughts. The basic idea is supported by an understructure of information.

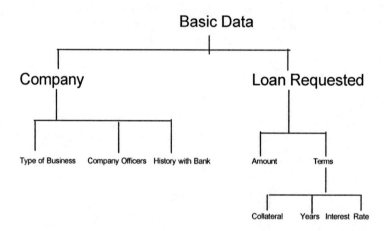

Consider the implications of this sort of structure of a talk. When you are planning it, you have only a few key points to keep in mind. As you present data in these organized chunks, you can easily keep in mind what the point is as you speak. You know how facts and thoughts relate to one another, both horizontally and vertically.

Most important of all, you have immense flexibility in four dimensions.

First, the sequence is easily altered. Because your talk is modular, you can easily re-arrange the order in which you present pieces. If the loan committee wants to hear about the potential problems and mitigants before addressing the terms of the loan, it is easily done. Instead of going 1, 2, 3, you count 2, 3, 1. Nothing could be simpler, and you will not get confused because the pieces are independent.

Even more valuable is the ability to expand and contract a talk according to time pressures. You just go deeper or less deep into the triangle.

Just before I was introduced to give a major speech, the moderator of the series said, "So, an hour talk and thirty minutes Q & A." When I replied that I had been told to prepare for a thirty-minute presentation with fifteen minutes of questions and answers, he replied, "Oh, I thought I'd told you. We switched the format." With that, he introduced me and I had to get up and begin with no more notice than that to double my speaking time.

It was easy to do.

My talk consisted of an introduction, five points, and a conclusion. I kept the opening and closing remarks unchanged and expanded each of the five points from four minutes apiece to ten minutes. I knew lots about the topic, so I could easily elaborate on my five points, and the structure even allowed me to keep on pace so I neither rushed nor padded the final point and could end on the dot of time.

Conversely, a three-hour presentation was, on the spot, required to fit into ninety minutes. If I went over, the audience would miss their tee times, so brevity was life and death. I merely needed to stay in the upper area of the triangles of my points and they heard the essentials of what I had to say. We did not go into as much detail as I had planned, but nothing important was missed, including the first tee.

Third, it solves the problem of speaking to an audience of people whose knowledge and interest in a topic varies greatly. These horizontally arranged triangles allow you to give two talks simultaneously! When you get to each point, you give the tip of it to the entire audience.[6] You then proceed to give the details to those who need or want them. The remainder of the audience will know generally what you are talking about, so they do not get bored or lost, but will realize that this is a level of complexity they do not need to understand fully. When you get to the next triangle, they can listen to that tip and then relax, letting the details wash past them.

For example, a small company, involved in a lawsuit, agrees to mediation to resolve the dispute. After hearing both sides, the mediator meets with the president of the company and her attorneys. The mediator needs to tell the president the practical meaning of his findings to date, but needs to let the lawyers know what legal precedents shaped those finding. The attorneys need to know the basis of the mediator's thinking so they can advise their boss; the president only needs to know what the mediator is saying, not why.

Fourth, the value of this approach is seen in the handling larger pieces as well.

Group or team presentations are commonplace and can be facilitated by imagining the process as a long journey broken into stages. The entire team is engaged in bringing the listeners from a starting point to a destination. In order to do so, the journey has been broken up into stages. Imagine a group of drivers bringing a passenger from New York to Los Angeles. The first driver takes him as far as Syracuse, where they meet a second driver who will bring him to Cleveland. The third goes to Chicago, the fourth to St. Louis, and so forth across the continent. Each member of the driving team has responsibility for a specific leg of the journey. The responsibility of each presenter is to meet the preceding speaker to pick up the audience and bring them along the next set of points to his or her destination, where the next member of the team is waiting. It is all rather like a relay race, with the audience as the baton.

A series of lectures, whether by an individual or a group, similarly fits this expanded journey metaphor. A very long presentation can be similarly broken down. Just as with the simple use of the horizontal technique for presenting, the key is the combination of short-term goals to meet a long-term goal.

And unlike real cross-country drivers, the points along the way in a horizontal presentation are virtual ones and so can be rearranged to change the sequence or add and eliminate points along the way as the needs of the audience are discovered in the course of the journey.

This organization also makes Q&A easy to handle.

When you are asked a question, understanding how to give an answer is built into the horizontal and vertical structure of your talk. Questions tend to fall into seven categories.

Perhaps most common are questions that request you to repeat what you already said. Usually this means re-wording your original statement, perhaps using examples or metaphors, to help the listener to understand what was missed originally.

Many questions request information in greater detail than you provided initially. In that case, you need merely go to the appropriate point along the horizontal series and go deeper into that triangle in order to add the requisite depth of detail.

The flip side of the second type of question is one where the listener has gotten bogged down in details and needs to have the main point of the triangle summarized. This may involve the main point of the talk or the tip of a point along the way.

Some questions understand the points of the horizontal organization but request clarification of the connections between them. One need merely expand upon the connections between points.

The next two types of question are closely related, differing in direction. Some ask you to go to before the starting point of your talk, giving more background about how you got to your beginning. Others seek to go beyond your destination, requesting you move on to the next talk. In both cases, you can think of two metaphors to guide you. You can use the image of a series of horizontal presentations, like a relay race, or else you can think vertically, and remember that every triangle is part of a larger one and so expand your thinking.

The final type of question is one for which you do not have an answer. There are three sub-types. You cannot answer some questions because the questioner is basing the query on an inaccurate premise. "If the earth is flat, how can a satellite go around it?" Some questions are simply out to lunch. "Michael, how long is your tongue?"

And others request information that is real and reasonable, but you do not know the answer. It lies in the area beyond your knowledge. Remember, no matter how much you know, there are always limits to your knowledge. These questions are frequently called "unexpected" because you do not know the answer. But if you expected them, you would have found out the answer in advance. There can always be unexpected questions. All you can do is to know as much as you can in advance, and respond by talking about what you do know plus promising to find out the precise information requested.

With these skills of presenting the information you already know vertically and horizontally, you are ready to go on to deliver your talk.

Chapter Eleven

Remembering What To Say

You may well have noticed what the effect of horizontal and vertical organization of your topic has on remembering what you want to say. It makes it easy.

Some people try to memorize a talk. This is a terrible strategy.

First of all, it takes forever. Who has the kind of time available to write out a verbatim transcript in advance, much less to memorize it?

And besides, if you did memorize it, you would have this patter all set to deliver but fragile and easily shattered. Think of those telemarketers who call, usually at dinnertime, to sell you some timesharing resort. They have the talk down cold, and as soon as you interrupt, they have to go back and find their places, as they do not know what they are really saying. They are like parrots, reciting lines devoid of meaning.

There are people who are trained to memorize large chunks of text. They are called actors and actresses. Not only are they skilled in learning lines, they also know how to deliver them in a fresh and lively manner. The odds are great that if you memorize your talk verbatim, you will deliver it like a robot, stiff and lifeless.

And to top it all off, trying to deliver a word-perfect recital would make anyone nervous. So much room for error, so many words to mess up. Ouch!

So, let's look at the alternative.

You know the point you are trying to get across. You know where your audience is and where you are trying to lead them. So far, so good. You could hardly forget that. Now what?

You have a small number of main points you want to address. This is why you do not have a horde of points. They would be too many to remember, too many opportunities to forget. You may have hundreds of ideas to get across, but you have clustered them. They fit together into little triangles. Once you remember the point, you automatically are reminded of what goes under it. If you have too many points, that means that you do not have a clear enough idea of the organization and your audience will have too many opportunities to lose you. So if you have too many points, bundle them.[7]

Now you only have a very small number of points to remember. This should be easy to do. They should fit together logically and fit into the overview you have created, so you can remember these few topics. Again, so far, so good.

Now each of these topics has bits and ideas associated with it. You will find that it is quite easy to remember what thoughts are connected to the tip of the triangle. Think back to last chapter. What goes under "terms of the loan?" You probably recall that this would be "collateral, years, and interest rate." See how easy it is to remember? And you probably are not a loan officer. Think how easy it would be to remember that if it were your field.

So you know that once you are on a topic, you can remember what goes beneath it in the triangle. The cascade of ideas is natural and makes sense. You are not dealing with rote memorization but instead with ideas that follow from one another.

Sometimes people worry that the whole thing gets too complex and overwhelming. That is because they lose sight of what they are doing. First of all, when you remember your vertical organization, you realize that everything has a place and the subsequent sense of order makes understanding even complex ideas easy. Second, when you think of horizontal presentation of topics, you realize that you have a small number of ideas to sequence. It is not hard if you take it step at a time.

Here is an example. Think of the last two numbers of your ten-digit home telephone number. Okay? If you are like almost everyone, you started at the beginning and said the whole thing in your mind till you got to the final digits. You do not really know them in a vacuum, but only as part of a larger structure. Start saying the whole number and when you get to the last two, there they are, waiting for you! You just start with confidence and when the time comes, you will know them.

When you talk, the same thing is true. Once you have structured your presentation horizontally and vertically, you are ready to begin. When you are on the second point, you do not need to have immediate mental access to the fourth point. In fact, you should not be thinking about the fourth step. That would only distract you from the one you are working on. Stay in the present. When you finish the third point, you will find the fourth one sitting there waiting for you.

So also with sub-points. Once you start talking about a point, the pieces that cascade from it will be there, ready for you to address. All you need to do is trust in your organization and stay in the present.

That is how to memorize a talk.

Chapter Twelve

Making a Talk Your Own

In business, people are frequently asked to deliver talks that have been prepared by someone else. Sometimes they are even asked to make a presentation that has previously been given by a co-worker. Sometimes, a script is prepared for several people to use. These scenarios create a typical set of problems that can be easily addressed.

There are musical groups that make their living copying the works of other bands. The number of Elvis impersonators is vast. There are many groups, with names like Beatlemania, Rubber Soul, the Silver Beatles, Fab Mania, and Yesterday, who make their living trying to sound like the original Beatles. Personally, I never understood the appeal. If I wanted to hear the Beatles, I would buy the CD and listen to the real thing. Mimicry as an art form seems to be something that is interesting to the extent that someone can do it, but it is a shallow art.

On the other hand, musicians who value their own ability sometimes record versions of songs that were originally released by other artists.[8] When they do, they do not slavishly copy the original but rather perform their own fresh version of the music. They make it their own.

In the world of classical music the situation is even more

pronounced. The best musicians play the same works. Beethoven, Mozart, Schumann, Listz, and Prokofiev as well as other composers in the canon are performed and recorded repeatedly by different artists. Each tries to give his or her own interpretation of the piece. If you told Pablo Casals and Yo-Yo Ma that they sounded alike, neither would be complimented. Good musicians take pride in their individuality.

When you are giving a talk, the last thing you should want to do is to sound like someone else. You are not that person, why should you expect to sound like him or her. Everyone has a particular set of strengths; you should emphasize yours, not demonstrate that you are a weak copy of someone else.[9]

So now that you know that you have to deliver your own version of the talk, how do you do it?

By going back to the start and re-making it.

When you get someone else's talk, you must figure out what the point of the talk is. What is the vertical organization? Next comes the horizontal preparation. You have to decide where it is trying to take the audience. More precisely, you must decide where you are trying to take the audience with this talk. Then you figure our where the audience is at the start. Finally, you have to take the pieces of the talk and arrange them into the main points along the way. You need to take the many pieces you have been given and clump them together until you have reduced it to a handful of main steps to the end. In other words, you need to take it apart to make certain you understand it, then put it back together again.

A particular example of this is seen with PowerPoint decks. In any set of slides, no matter how large, each one is not equally important and they do not stand alone. When you go through them, you see that they form natural clusters. Perhaps the first ten slides might be about company history; the next ten about the larger market, the following twenty about a new product, and the final six about the financials. Forty-six slides condensed to four main points.

An illustration.

An investment-banking firm had put together an all-day meeting with prospective investors for a company that had revolutionized the supply process in their industry. The bankers had mapped out presentations by all the chief officers of the firm, complete with PowerPoint slides. When the CFO began to do his part in practice, he arrived at a group of slides that detailed the successes of a client company. He knew the field well and could talk eloquently about the client's achievements, but it was totally detached from the rest of his talk, a distraction.

I asked him why he was telling about this company and he admitted that he had no idea, except that it was part of his deck. When we took the talk apart, it was obvious that this vignette was put there as an example of the way that his firm's supply process could bring increased profitability to its customers and so showed the viability of the business model.

When he went through the talk a second time, the inclusion made sense, both to him and to his audience. He understood what he was saying, not merely parroting what he had been given to say.

You need to go through the work of de-constructing the presentation, seeing what it says and how it says it, and put it back together to fit your personality and style.

Note that this does not necessarily need to mean that you are totally in agreement with the contents of the talk. Your personal opinion may be totally at variance with the talk you have been given.

The secret is to realize the difference between speaking as an individual versus speaking in your role in an organization. If you are announcing a company policy to the people you manage, to add as a sidebar that you do not agree with company policy is to court disaster. By giving contradictory messages of official policy and your individual opinion, you have placed your employees in a no-win situation. If they follow policy they are oposing you. If they follow your heart, they are counter corporate policy.

Whether you personally agree or not, you need to take on the persona of your role in order to deliver the message convincingly.

Chapter Thirteen

The Beginning

There are sets of mathematical problems that are said to be incalculable. It is not necessarily that they are so difficult to compute but that there are so many calculations involved as to be unworkable.

For example, when computers are programmed to play chess, it would seem that the sure-fire way to win would be to merely go through all the possible moves and see which ones ended up in winning final positions. In theory there is nothing wrong with this. In fact, it would allow you to see every possible outcome and every possible combination of moves.[10]

The problem is that there are just too many moves. White has twenty possible first moves and Black has twenty possible responses. That means there are four hundred possible positions after the first move. Opening up the board with the first move means that there are many more than twenty possible second moves for both White and Black, and the explosion of possibilities is just beginning. It is estimated that there are 10^{120} (1 followed by 120 zeros) possible moves. By comparison, there are estimated to be 10^{75} atoms in the entire universe! If you assigned one move per atom you would not have nearly enough to do the job. So while in theory it is not difficult to plan out all the possible moves, *a la* tic-tac-toe, in practice it is impossible. The number of possibilities makes the calculation process impossible, hence incalculable.

When planning out a talk, it is impossible to plan for all of the possible scenarios, including questions, interruptions, and the like. If you were an actor with a verbatim script and the cooperation of everyone else, also actors, involved it would not be difficult, but we are assuming you do not live in Movieland. You cannot prepare for every eventuality. There are too many branchings to the possibility tree.

But the beginning of a talk is something you can predict and control. It is your chance to connect with the listener and interest him or her in following you on your journey. The beginning is small enough to be crafted. It can be a jewel that sets the tone for an interesting journey together. It is worth expending extra energy to create this great start.

Remembering that the start of horizontal presenting is to go to where the audience is, the first key to the beginning is to say something that makes that initial connection. There are many ways of doing this, and none is always the best choice for every situation.

There is a school of presenting often described as "Tell them what you're going to tell them, tell them, and then tell them what you told them." This has a certain sort of straightforward simplicity and it can work well in certain sorts of encounters, primarily training situations and data dumps with a captive audience. This approach is trying to do explicitly what the organizational techniques of this book do somewhat more subtly: make access to the information easy and clear.

There are two problems with this approach. The first is that a non-captive audience may think, "Why should I care?" and not pay attention. A variation of this failure is that the audience, hearing the "What I'm going to tell you," will mentally respond, "Okay, that tells me all I want to know about that topic," and will then tune out.

The second problem is a subtler one. Not only at the beginning of your talk but almost always, your job is to *tell* them the story, not to tell them what you are going to do. If you think about it, any time you are telling them what you are going to do is time spent not doing it! Sometimes it can be useful to explain where you are taking them, but long statements of what you will do are generally to be avoided.

Some openings are simple. If you have a motivated audience and a clear subject, you can just march right into the meat. "Our profits have increased in each of the last five quarters." "Mom, Dad, I'm married." "We, the jury, find the defendant..." Other talks require getting the interest of your listeners before you can hold it.

A related sort of opening is to begin *in medias res*, in the middle of things. Stories with well-known characters, whether historical or in the news, can tap into a reservoir of experience and memory that bonds speaker and audience. "One day, when Robin Hood was hunting in Sherwood Forest..." "The latest version of Windows has again raised questions about Bill Gates' desire to gain control..." "The rage of Achilles, sing about that, Goddess..." "The Federal Reserve Bank announced today that interest rates..."

In a related way, sometimes you can invite the listeners into a magical world and the ritual invocation is enough to get them to suspend disbelief willingly. "Once upon a time, there was a beautiful princess..." "Long ago, in a galaxy far, far away..." These sorts of openings alert the audience to a changed reality and, if the invitation is accepted, open their minds to fantasy.

Sometimes you might want to open by talking about what has been happening in the room. "That certainly was an inspiring story we just heard about little Bobby and his dog Tiger." "I know it has been a long morning and I know that everyone is eager to get out on the golf course, so I will be brief. The outlook for Q3 is...." "I am sorry that the sprinkler system accidentally went off and soaked everyone, but perhaps that will make everyone a little more aware of the importance of our next topic, fire safety."

Former president Clinton was a master at personalizing talks this way. When he would attend a political dinner on campaign stop, he would talk to the locals when he arrived, gathering tidbits of information about people in the crowd and happenings in the town. When it was time for him to speak, he would begin by making reference to the various items of harmless gossip he had picked up, commenting on the mayor's birthday or the recent Squash Festival in the town square. The effect was galvanizing, as people felt he really knew and cared all about them. He could then move into his boilerplate standard campaign speech and they not only kept listening, but they also continued to feel it was addressed specifically to them. The initial opening was priceless, for it got everyone to agree to come along with him.

An opening that introduces or strengthens a bond of identification with the audience can be extremely effective. The use of "We" can impart a sense of fellowship or kinship that establishes the relationship between speaker and audience. This can be formulaic, as when the President begins "My fellow Americans," or extremely moving, as when Father Damien first addressed the patients on Molokai as "My fellow lepers." Sometimes, when the connection is not obvious, a speaker may begin "I remember when I was your age, eager and ready to go out and change the world..." She lets them know that while she is no longer young, she remembers when she was. As with the boy who fell from his bike, the message is "I understand who you are and how you feel, so now come along from there with me."

One popular sort of opening is to begin with a question or a series of questions. Do so at your own peril. Think back to the movie *Ferris Bueller's Day Off.* Remember the teacher, who, having asked a question of an unresponsive class, was reduced to droning, "Anyone? Anyone?" To open with a question is to invite the audience to give a live demonstration of how little relationship you have with them. All they have to do is be passive and you are hung out to dry, twisting in the breeze.

If you really want to open with questions, there are two ways to minimize the dangers of putting yourself at their mercy. First, ask questions that require little energy of the audience and that do not ask them to reveal too much. Compare "Are we all convinced that our company has a superior product?" to, "So, who is looking to quit and take a job with our competitor?" Make it easier for your audience to interact than it is for them to play dumb. Another useful technique is to be prepared to turn your question into a rhetorical one. "What is the outlook for sales in the next quarter?" (Pause long enough to give anyone who might wish to reply a chance to do so, but not so long as to make it clear you are hoping for an answer.) "The outlook is good," said strongly and as if you had been planning to answer it yourself all along. If you get an answer, you have an interaction. If not, you were not looking for one anyway.

Some others have learned to open with a joke. You probably are not funny enough to do that. The best most people can muster is to repeat a joke they heard someone else tell. If you are really that funny, there is a great deal of money to be made doing comedy professionally and you should explore that as a career move. But even the pros do not just go up and tell jokes. They work and re-work material to get it right, particularly the timing, which is crucial to humor. Notice how most people who try to open with a joke seem pretty flat. There really is a refined skill set to humor. (Besides, most of the funny stories are probably going to offend someone, anyway, so who needs that headache.) This is not at all to suggest that you stifle your natural ability to be humorous. By all means, let your natural wit shine forth. Just do not try to be another Henny Youngman.

A story, parable, or metaphor can be an excellent beginning, particularly to a dry topic or one that might intimidate people. The idea is to begin talking about something people understand, to which they can relate, and then use it as a springboard to the actual topic. I remember a woman who began by telling about going to the local sandwich shop to get her lunch. On impulse, she bought a scratch ticket for a dollar and when she had rubbed it, learned that she had won a dollar back. "I thought to myself,' she continued," wouldn't it be great if you could invest money with the possibility of winning a lot but with a guarantee that at worst, you would get all your money back?" At that point she had piqued everyone's curiosity and we listened as she went on to tell us about some sort of life insurance policy that paid you back your premiums paid if you did not die.

The advantage of such an opening is that it gives an insight into a topic that may not be evident. Many people do not understand the intricacies of underwriting; nearly everyone has tried a scratch ticket. It can be especially effective as a means of circumventing defenses to deliver bad news. Think of the Biblical story of the prophet Nathan telling mighty King David about a rich man who had robbed a poor man. Hearing this beginning, David was enraged at the miscreant. When Nathan identified the man as David himself, for taking Bathsheeba from Uriah the Hittite, David heard the rest. If Nathan had begun by saying, "Let's talk about your crimes and sins, Oh King," the royal reception would have been far less inviting.

A speaker who is not well or personally known to the audience often finds advantage in telling a little story about her or himself. Whether it reveals roots or recent experiences, it makes the listeners more willing to go along on your journey because you are not a stranger anymore.

Finally, opening words such as "Good morning," or, "It's a pleasure to be here," can best be thought of as conventions that announce that you are about to speak. They are similar to the lights going down in a concert hall. That is not the beginning of the music but rather a sign to sit down and shut up, because the performance is about to begin.

The opening lines of your talk, then, can be much more carefully crafted than the body of the talk and have the task of interesting your listeners enough that they will go with you to your first point.

Chapter Fourteen

The Ending

The talk is almost fully crafted. All that is lacking is the ending.

Like the beginning, the ending can be well crafted. As on a journey, while the middle of the trip presents many options, your first few steps and the final arrival should be pretty much set. You need to have a good closing that does two things.

First of all, you need to let the audience know you are done. In a play, they bring down the curtain. In a movie, they roll the credits. At a football game they fire a pistol. In basketball they sound a horn. You know the show is over. It is finished. Think of bad speakers you have heard, who go along and then abruptly stop talking. You have an embarrassed few seconds wondering if they forgot the next point, then you realize it is over. Spare your audience that wondering. Let them know you have arrived at the destination.

One way of doing so is to use one of the standard verbal equivalents of the curtain fall. "Thank you." "Are there any questions?" "I will be available later to meet with anyone who would like to pursue this." All of these are signals of the end.

While the audience can thus get the message "Game Over," it can be abrupt if not well crafted. That is why second, and more importantly, your ending needs to be satisfying, giving the listener a sense of completeness.

Shakespeare frequently ended scenes and acts by making the last two lines rhyme. The couplet let everyone know it was time to move on. Think back to good movies and plays you have seen. The ending has to give you a sense of wholeness. This does not mean that it cannot contain seeds of a sequel, but there has to be a sense of reaching a destination.

A common device is to refer back to the beginning and demonstrate how far you have come and that the initial goals have been met. A related device is to conclude with a call for action, typically the action first described in the opening lines.

The antithesis of a satisfying close is one where the speaker gets to the end and drifts around, saying vague things like "So there we are. I guess that's about it. It really is a pretty good product. I think it's pretty good…"

Think of pieces of music you know and compare those which end with a clear, sharp finish to those which drift through repetitions and finally fade away as a substitute for concluding.

You have taken your audience of a journey. You need to be ready to let them know definitively when you have arrived.

Your technical and content preparation is complete.

Chapter Fifteen

On to the Second Pillar

Now you know how to organize your talk, how to begin, and how to end. You have the technical information you need. Now it is time to work on yourself, on who you are in the presenting situation.

The first thing you need to have and keep in your mind when you are about to speak, and while you are speaking, is that you are an expert.

You know something that your audience needs to hear. You have knowledge that you are going to impart. Even if you tend to feel insecure and doubtful, you need to understand the value you can bring to the discussion. Take the time to think about it. If you do not think you have something valuable to tell the audience, then for goodness sake sit down and shut up. There are too many noisy people already. If you have nothing worth saying, take to heart the truism "Better to keep quiet and have people think you are ignorant than to open your mouth and remove all doubt." That's right, if you really think you have nothing to add, be quiet. But if you have something, do not lose sight of the value of your expert contribution.

People who have a phobia usually believe there is some reality basis to their fear. Before they can overcome their fear they must decide it is safe to do so. For example, one cannot conquer a fear of flying until you decide that airplanes are safe enough to risk. In the same way, you cannot overcome a feeling that you have nothing worth saying until you look and see that you do indeed have knowledge worth sharing.

But you know you have some degree of expertise. You do not know everything in the world about everything, but you have your area of competence. Remember the mapping of your area of knowledge in Chapter Three.

When a copy of the first article I ever published arrived in the mail, I opened the journal to the table of contents and saw it there, my name and the title. I had a moment of panic, thinking "Someone reading this might think I know as much about my subject as the other 'real' authors do about theirs." Fortunately for my future sense of expertise, my follow-up thought was "I probably do, and they probably realize their knowledge is limited, just as mine is."

The final hurdle for graduate students at university is to defend a dissertation. For this final book-length work, the student must become the expert on a tiny area of knowledge. Once it is written, he or she goes before a committee of professors to "defend" it. The basic idea is that the professors, as senior scholars in the field, know more than the student about the field as a whole. However, the student is expected to know more about his or her topic than anybody, including the faculty members.

A major financial institution has a policy of choosing six of their newly hired MBAs every year and assigning them to different areas of the firm. At the end of a year, they are brought before the presidents of the various companies that constitute the giant firm and are expected to tell how the firm appeared to them. Now, obviously, they do not have the overview, depth, or long-term vision of the company that the presidents do. However, the presidents can learn what they could not see themselves: how the company looks from the new MBA point of view. The firm wants to safeguard itself from an Emperor's New Clothes problem and it puts these junior executives in the role of the child.

They know what the presidents do not and could not, so they are the experts in that setting and have something valuable to contribute.

As soon as you begin to speak, you are automatically granted some degree of expert status; they are listening to you, after all. It may be grudging or admiring, respectful or resentful, but they are willing to listen to you. They are granting you *de facto* expert status. You have the floor. You are an expert.

The second thing you need to keep in mind is that you are a partner to the listeners. You are not an enemy, not an adversary, not an ordeal, not a necessary evil, but a partner. You are there to bring your fellow travelers to the destination. This is true whether you are speaking to people who are glad to hear your message or to those who are not. Your job is to work with them, even if they wish you were going elsewhere.

The destination affects the he nature of the interaction. If you were physically leading children from one place to another, there would be differences between a trip to the toy or candy store, a trip to the doctor's for injections, and a trip to a soccer game. In all these cases, however, you would be leading partners where they need to go.

Sometimes the interaction is a simple transmission of information. This is commonly seen in some cases of delivering financial reports or giving technical specifications of a product, where the goal is to provide impersonal, impartial data. In these instances, you would do well to think of your role as analogous to the weatherman. The weather forecaster does not make it rain or shine. She merely reports what nature has provided. You are simply telling what the numbers are, not what you wish they were or why they are. You are the friendly, neighborhood information source.

Frequently, a talk has a persuasive element. Then you are not merely an impartial partner but also an inspirational one, trying to motivate them to agree with you and your vision.

Sometimes you are seeking information, trying to develop a dialogue with your listeners. In this case, the need for cooperative interaction is evident.

Whatever the situation, you need to remember "You cannot be in two places at once." That is the law in presenting as well as in physics. You can't physically be at the podium and sitting in the audience. You can't be mentally in two places either. You can't be presenting and listening to yourself. Trying to do both means doing neither well. Don't listen to yourself speak. You pay attention to the talking and let the listeners do the listening.

In all of these cases, you need to keep fixed in your mind that you are an expert and a partner. You have a tale to tell, with a beginning, middle, and an ending.

You are a storyteller. Tell your story.

Chapter Sixteen

Our Inherited Problem

In his work *On the Origin of Species,* Charles Darwin described the evolutionary interaction between an environment and the development of traits that promote survival in that setting. Individuals possessing characteristics that made them less likely to be killed were more likely to have descendants who would possess the same genes and survival traits.

Two million years ago, our earliest ancestors appeared on the plains of Africa. Archeologists have found the remains of many of them, including one found at Olduvai Gorge in Tanzania dubbed "Lucy."

These earliest proto-humans were relatively small and weak. They lived in a world filled with predators, who would seek to devour them, and other tribes of humans, who would compete for resources such as and food and shelter. The competition for existence was physical and violent; the arts of negotiation, debate, and passive resistance had not yet evolved. For Lucy and her kinfolk, evolution favored the strongest, those gifted with physical skills.

It is rare, perhaps unknown, to be so physically dominant that threats are negligible. Even the King of the Beasts, who may sleep for up to twenty hours per day, faces challenges from other lions in the competition for mates. It requires a significant expenditure of resources to be ready to handle a physical threat, more than can be sustained over time. But an individual who is asleep or relaxed is not well prepared to deal with an attack.

A solution developed by many animals, including lions and humans, is the "fight or flight response," the biological equivalent of quickly going to "battle stations." This allows the creature to conserve resources in periods of safety, yet remain ready to go all out quickly in time of danger.

For humans, like all mammals, a primitive area deep in the brain, called the limbic system, triggers this response. When the fight or flight response is activated, adrenaline pours into the bloodstream. The pupils of the eyes dilate to enhance vision. The bloodstream supplies extra oxygen to the muscles to allow maximum exertion. Blood to the skin is cut off, to reduce bleeding if wounded. Hair stands on end (gooseflesh) to make the person appear larger and more frightening, much as a cat does. The body is then ready for combat or to flee. The ability to switch into this high-energy mode had definite survival advantages for Lucy and her kin. A key to understanding the fight or flight response is that it is not triggered by the actual manifestation of danger but merely by the perception of a threat. As soon as danger is deemed likely, adrenaline kicks in.

Our bodies continued to evolve, reaching our current form about one hundred thousand years ago. The human brain added layers capable of higher thought, but the old Lucy brain with the limbic system remained inside. This was quite appropriate, because the world remained a predominantly physically threatening place until quite recently.

The Lucy part of the brain is still present today. It has its uses. Physical threats do occur. Accidents happen, attacks, while uncommon, do occur, and when they do, the fight or flight response is there to make us ready.

But in recent centuries, human society and technology have evolved at a much faster rate than human bodies. Wild beasts are rare. We are more likely to make a killing in the stock market than in the forest. The trial by jury has replaced trial by combat. Even when we do fight wars, we use guns and missiles rather than rocks and sticks. It is a world where we rule by thinking rather than by hitting. We use the cerebral cortex more than our fists. We do face threats and dangers, but they rarely are physical ones. Battling a hostile take-over requires a different set of tools than repelling a besieging army. Even back when the fighting was physical, as in *The Iliad*, thinking is crucial. The deciding factor in that war was the Trojan Horse.

Jump forward to the present day business world. A person at a business dinner is called upon to speak. He feels apprehension. His Lucy instinct triggers the fight or flight response. He is primed to run from the podium or to grab a butter knife and attack his boss. Neither is a good career move. He is a mass of explosive physical energy trying to deliver a reasoned argument to his audience. He has instinctively but unproductively put himself in a state that hurts rather than helps him.

The problem is that the instincts that humans developed in Lucy's era make us prone to respond to fear by triggering the limbic system, preparing us for a physical response to a non-physical situation. Our environment has evolved faster than our instincts.

There is a solution. It lies in the ability of our more modern brain to over-ride our instincts. We do not have to respond instinctively. Impulse does not have to become manifest in action. The secret is to keep the conscious brain in control.

Instincts cannot be honored as the final arbiter of action.

A fire in a stable is a terrible thing, made far worse by the horses' instinctive fear of fire. Confronted with fire, a horse will pull away in terror. If there were an open stable door but the frame was blazing with fire, a horse would be too terrified to go through it, even though safety was visible beyond the flames. Its instinctive fear of fire would immobilize it. Stable hands know to cover the horse's eyes with a blanket. When it cannot see the fire, it can be led to safety.

Thoroughbreds are wonderful animals, but they are not very smart. They act on instinct, not on free-will choice. Animal behavior is dictated by instincts, but human behavior is only suggested by them. We not only have the limbic system but also the cerebral cortex, the thinking part of the brain. Like the human stable hands who rescue the horses, the cortex can over-ride the instinctive anxiety response.

Chapter Seventeen

Your Body

The interaction between your mind and your body is worth understanding. What affects one affects the other and the system is bi-directional. This means that when your mind is tense, your muscles become tense as well. When your mind is relaxed, so is your body.

Interestingly enough, the system works in the other direction just as well. If your muscles are tense, your mind will follow suit and if you relax your muscles, your mind will relax as well. Valium is thought of as a tranquilizer, but its mode of operation is as a muscle relaxant. That is why people take it for back spasms. A person taking Valium will have muscles so relaxed that the mind will think, "Things must be safe. If there were any danger, my muscles would be tense."

One secret of staying relaxed is to remember that the muscles involved are voluntary ones. You can choose to relax them. You can order your arms and legs, hands and feet, back, chest and abdomen, neck and jaw muscles to relax. You can drain the tension out of them.

You know you can do this because you know that you are physically safe. You do not need to use the fight or flight response. There is no danger.

Sometimes a person feels too tense to relax. If that happens, there is a trick to relaxation.

When a horse gets the bit in his teeth and begins to run away, a rider is taught not to fight the horse. The horse is the stronger, and futilely ordering him to stop only reminds him that he is in command. Instead, the rider orders her horse to "giddy-up" and run faster! As this is what the horse was already doing, he will automatically obey. The rider is then seen to be giving the orders that are obeyed. When, a little later, she orders the horse to slow down, he does so. She is the boss.

So with your body. If your muscles are tense and difficult to relax, order them to tense. When you next order relaxation, they will, because the locus of control has been re-affirmed.

If you find your body shaking or quivering with tension, that means that adrenaline has already entered the system. First you need to shut down the fight or flight response to keep more adrenaline from entering the bloodstream, then you need to deal with what is already there. The best way to get rid of it is to exercise your muscles. Vigorous exercise, like jumping jacks, is ideal but often impractical. A more likely possible alternative is to do isometrics or tense and relax exercises. Adrenaline is there to boost physical performance, so activity will use it up.

Once you are physically relaxed, it will be easier to keep your mind relaxed and so able to focus on the task at hand.

Some people feel exposed when they are speaking, particularly if they have to stand up in front of the audience. They feel (and some-times look) like a deer in the headlights. They feel exposed and vul-nerable.

There are two complementary tricks to help with that. The first method makes use of the technique of exaggeration to absurdity, the second uses changing the name to change the attitude.

First, imagine getting up in front of an audience holding a target in front of your chest. (See illustration.) Imagine that everyone is thus encouraged to take aim at you. The target is tempting, taunting, invit-ing the audience to open fire. But you realize "Open fire with what?" They are not armed. There is no physical threat. Perhaps the audi-ence might wad up paper and throw it at you. So what? You are not in any genuine danger. Quite literally, in the words of FDR, you have "nothing to fear but fear itself." What they might throw at you are questions. They might be directing their attention towards you. That would be all right. And you know that the best way to prepare for questions, particularly difficult questions, is to be physically relaxed and mentally sharp.

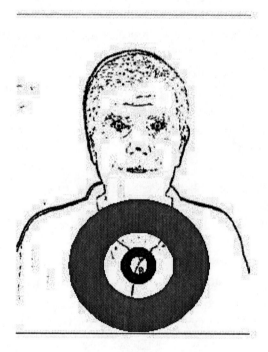

The second trick is to re-name the feeling to one of being in the spotlight. You are the star. Everyone wants to hear and see you. This is a good thing. It gives you the possibility of getting people to understand your position and to be convinced by you. This is your opportunity to make a difference. You are a thoroughbred who wants to lead the herd.

An idea that cannot be overstated is that you must hold onto the idea that this is not anxiety; this is excitement.

A little girl went on a roller coaster with a slightly older friend, whose mother was rather overprotective. During the ride, both girls screamed, as many people do on the roller coaster, and at the conclusion were flushed and excited. "Wasn't that terrible? Weren't you scared? Didn't you hate it?" asked the mother.

"Yes," said her daughter, "It was horrible. I was so scared."

"And weren't you scared, too?" she demanded of the little girl.

The girl looked at her older friend, who understood that what she had felt was fear, and then at her father, who simply said, "It sure looked as if you were having fun. You tell me."

"It was great," said the little girl. "I had a great time. It was so exciting."

She grew up to be very brave.

In the musical *The King and I,* Anna is frightened at the prospect of going to a foreign land and reveals her strategy, singing

> "Whenever I feel afraid,
> I hold my head erect
> And whistle a happy tune
> So no one will suspect I'm afraid…
> The result of this deception
> Is very strange to tell,
> For when I fool the people I meet,
> I fool myself as well."

The successful strategy not only does the task of hiding her fears from others, it makes her feel brave indeed.

Feelings are not mystical emanations from some unknowable ethereal plane. They occur in your brain, a complicated but understood collection of nerve cells. Feelings and emotions, including fear, anxiety, confidence, and courage, are the product of the interaction of thought and action. If your intellect and behavior are those of a brave person or a coward, a confident person or an insecure one, your emotions will follow accordingly.

It does not work to say, "I'm really afraid, but I will go through the motions of saying 'I'm brave'," because what you are saying, stripped of the fluff, is, "I'm really afraid." You can be aware of the fact that your emotions have not yet caught up with your mind, that you are feeling nervous. But if you say, despite the evidence of your own guts, "I am brave and unafraid!" and act accordingly, you will quickly realize that you are, like Anna, in fact, unafraid.

Selling has a particular set of challenges, because the nature of the interaction makes rejection part of the process. It is useful to remember that you are not being found adequate or lacking, but rather discovering whether there is a fit between what you offer and what they need.

Shyness is genetic, at least in part. Scientists can examine an infant and determine whether he or she will grow up to be shy. But innate shyness is not destiny. Shy people can learn to be open, extroverts, just as naturally open people can learn to be shy and withdrawn. The secret is understanding that we are not horses or any other instinct driven animal. We can choose to go in counter-intuitive directions because we have a cerebral cortex to over-rule those instincts.

We have a smoke detector in our house. Sometimes, when we broil a steak, the molecules from the sizzling meat set off the alarm. When that happens, we could call 911 and go running from the house in terror for our lives, because the fire alarm has sounded, or we could make a quick check to see that there are no flames, then ignore the warning. We do the latter, because we know that the primitive sensors of the smoke alarm cannot distinguish between a burning house and a broiling sirloin. We use our intellects to over-rule our alarm system.

So also a successful presenter, even one born with the shyness gene, ignores the intuitive danger signal, and seizes the moment and the podium.

Chapter Eighteen

Handling Materials
(Don't Be Handled by Them)

There are a number of tips that are useful in the handling of supplementary materials, whether notes, handouts, PowerPoint slides, overheads, or any other aids to presenting. We will begin with those you might use for yourself and move to ones which you give or show to the audience.

Most important of all is to keep in mind that you are trying to show the audience that you have something to tell them. You are the storyteller. That means you have it in your head, and that means DO NOT READ. If you have a splendidly written paper, whose *mots* are all *tres bon*, still do not read it. The written word is not the spoken word. If you want to hand out a written document rather than talk to people, by all means do so. Just do not confuse the two and try to make a written document sound verbal. To present, you need to tell them what is in your head, not what is on paper.

One main point you wish to make is that you know the subject. If you have to read the material, that gives the impression that the script, not you, is the expert. If the paper is so perfect as to demand reading, you should hire someone else to read it, perhaps James Earl Jones.

His sculpted bass and his ability to use that voice as an instrument will make his reading better than yours. It does not matter that he does not know the content; he sure can read it well. If you read it, the twin messages your audience will receive at a subliminal level are that you do not really know your stuff and that you do not read aloud as well as a professional. (If you do read that well, you might consider a career in Hollywood. Let some screenwriter produce the scripts for you to read.)

Once you are not reading verbatim text, the next issue concerns your notes. In general, the less note dependent you are, the better. The more detailed your notes, the more opportunity for trouble. Remember that the more you have your talk structured in your mind, the easier it is to remember without help. Each part leads to the next and there is no need for written cues. These techniques make it easy to organize and remember a talk. Keep in mind that the fewer the notes you need, the more you and your audience will appreciate your knowledge. Trust yourself and your memory.

Like a scripted text, obvious reliance on notes delivers the message that you are not really able to handle delivering the message. Worse, it gives you the suggestion that you do not really know it.

One good use of notes, if they are needed at all, is to have them available but unused. Many people find it reassuring to know that if they need to refer to them, they could, but meanwhile, since they do not require a reminder, they ignore them. If you follow this path, do not fall into the "I've got them so I'll use them" trap.

If you do make notes, see how few words you can use to create them. The longer and more detailed the phrases you put in your notes, the more tempted you will be to read them in order to repeat a particularly apt turn of phrase. Remember, these notes do not have to make any sense to anyone else. They are memory aids for you alone, to remind you of what you already know.

Because they are for you alone, use abbreviations, pictures, or symbols that will jog your memory. Remember, they are designed to help you talk about the subject, not to take your place. If you know what it means, that is good enough. When in doubt, use too little rather than too much. Give yourself the chance to see that you do not need these memory aids.

One excellent technique for structuring your notes is to cut 8 ½" by 11" sheets of paper in half, orienting the new sheets so they are 5 ½ inches wide and 8 ½ inches in length. If available, use a lined pad, so you end up with sheets with lines running vertically down the page. This gives you a notes page that is narrow enough so your eyes can take in an entire line without moving from left to right. (Try it. See that on an ordinary piece of paper your eyes needs to move horizontally to cover a line on the page. On the half-page, your eyes need only scroll vertically. Consider how much easier it is to handle a web page with only a vertical nav bar than one with a horizontal bar as well.)

You want to have a descending series of (a few) reminders of what is already in your head. The lack of horizontal lines will keep you from feeling constrained to write notes of a certain size and length. Remember, some ideas are more major than others. Some words should be larger, bolder print, or in color. The only rule is that it must remind you of what is next in as little space as possible. The key to the successful use of notes is that you do not want to appear to be using notes, as far as is possible.

There are exceptions to this. For example, if giving detailed figures, it would be preferable to have them at your fingertips. Remember that in such an instance, where hard figures are available elsewhere, the verbal response is usually understood to be an approximation. ("We are forecasting gains of about 7%." "The overwhelming majority support the initiative.") If you cannot give a good enough approximation without notes, the next best is to say "That would be, let me see, here (looking at notes in a way that shows thorough familiarity with them by going straight to the appropriate part) ah yes, $12.46 million." (Note that here, where notes are consulted, it is preferable to add a bit of precision to the answer. This gives the impression that you knew the general answer but were unsure of the second decimal point. Knowing where in the data you could find the answer is another exhibition of competence.)

A very common error is to do housekeeping in the midst of a presentation. If you were at a podium speaking and you had been provided with a glass of ice water, you would pay no heed if condensation formed and made a ring on the wood. You certainly would not stop your speech and ask for a napkin to mop up the water. You are too busy making your points. Similarly, when you are talking, your notes, overheads, slides, and everything else you might employ do not need to be arranged for your next talk in the middle of this one. Do not worry about keeping used slides, notes, or visual aides in order. You or your assistant can straighten and order them later. Once you have used an overhead, toss it aside. Do not give the message that the most important thing in your mind is the neatness of the transparencies. You have seen other people do that and know that it makes the present talk devalued.

If you are using notes, remember that your job is still to be in contact with the audience. Glance down if you must to get your cue, then re-establish eye contact with your audience and talk to them.

There are two keys to remember when you reach the end of a page of notes. First, when you need to go from one page to the next, do not flip over the sheet you are finishing. On a related note, do not write on both sides of the sheet. To flip the note page over is to wave it around. Why not yell, "Look, I need notes!" As your goal is to make them inconspicuous, simply slide the used note to the side without lifting it from the podium and be ready for the next one.

Second, do not do this during a pause. When you get near to the end of a page of notes, get the final idea of the page in mind, look up at the audience and while you are speaking to them, making good eye contact, then you slide the spent page aside. Think of a magician who uses distraction to get the audience looking where he wants them to look. If you watch yourself moving pages, so will they. Practice sliding a sheet aside while looking away and talking. It's easy.

PowerPoint and other computer-based visual effects such as on-line demonstrations of software are a major source of temptation to many people to absent themselves from the storyteller role. Remember *The Wizard of Oz*? "Pay no attention to that little man behind the curtain!" Many like to use PowerPoint as a powerful presence to distract the audience away from the speaker. They try to get the audience to look at the beautiful slides and so allow the presenter to hide, like Oz, behind the curtain.

This is a major error.

First of all, it totally undermines your basic position and role as storyteller and guide. You *want* to be in front, telling the audience what you know.

Not only does this undermine your confidence in yourself, it eliminates your relationship with the audience. They are not getting the story from you. But this is a presentation, not merely a slide show. You need to relate with them.

Third, technology has been known to fail. Experienced presenters may find it hard to believe, but sometimes the magic does not work. The computer crashes, the LED projector does not arrive, the power fails.

You always need to be ready to present without your high-tech effects.

Besides, is there anything more conducive to a nice nap than sitting in a stuffy auditorium after lunch, with the lights dimmed and PowerPoint running, accompanied by a droning voice?

The best way to think of PowerPoint, video clips, demos, and all the panoply of high-tech presentation aids is as special effects. Good work by Industrial Light and Magic can make the fabulous look real on the screen, but it cannot make a movie good. A great movie tells a story. Special effects can help tell the story well, but they are no substitute for the foundation.

Overhead projections and PowerPoint can do some things better than your voice can. Use them effectively to do their job without letting them try to do yours.

For example, a graph can show an audience at a glance what it would take a thousand words to tell. Use visuals to give data this way. Let trends be seen in bar graphs and shares be shown in pie charts. If you want to use a slide to give data, even a huge spreadsheet, hold on to your role as guide. Tell them the point of the slide. For example, the tip of the triangle of a large table of data might be that the bottom line was profit, or that one-time expenses due to a system conversion was responsible for the bottom line loss, or that EBITDA is the key figure. Let the audience see that you are showing all the figures ("Nothing up my sleeves,") and then tell them what you see as the real story.

Most of all, NEVER READ ALOUD THE TEXT OF A POWERPOINT SLIDE!

Many companies like to do such things as put their mission statement early on in a deck. That is fine. Put it on the screen and let the audience read it. They are literate. They will read it themselves whether you read it aloud or not. In fact, they can read it silently faster than you can read it to them, so they will be done while you are still reading.

If you have read it to them, you have just demonstrated that you are irrelevant. They were done while you were still droning on. You taught them to ignore you. If you have to put up text slides, either simply let them read them or else say something about what it says. Paraphrase, emphasize a point, or make a comment. ("It's more than a slogan for us.") Just do not read it verbatim.

Handouts are another invitation to distraction. You need to be very careful in their use. You want to tell them your story, not have them read about it while they ignore you. If you do use them, guide the audience through them. Follow the same rules as with PowerPoint. If you want to have them examine a document, wait quietly while they do. Never get in competition with your own materials, because you are guaranteed to lose. When they have had enough time, reassert control and resume speaking.

A major variable in speaking is posture and position, sitting or standing, at a podium or on the move. Many people find one easy and the other hard, but all the variations are easy when you understand what the symbolism and meaning of each is. When you are at ease with the format, you reacquire your confidence.

The four basic positions for speaking are, in increasing level of formality, sitting, walking around, standing still, and standing at a podium.

Sitting, especially sitting at a table with your listeners, gives an atmosphere of informality and collegiality. No one is assuming a superior position and you are not "more exposed" as a target. The downside is that you do not get to send the body language message that you have the floor at this moment.

Walking around, whether across a stage, between desks of listeners, or in the audience, *a la* Oprah, simultaneously gives the impression that you are in charge (for only you are standing) with the informality and casual air of the peripatetic method. Socrates did this.

One advantage to this relaxation is that it makes it clear that you are working without notes or prompts and have everything you need in your head.

Standing lends authority, and standing in one spot adds to the seriousness and formality of your words. You are not casually walking but rather standing your ground, delivering an important message. You need to be comfortable with the assumption of authority implicit in your posture.

The podium is the most formal setting for presenting. It is a symbolic expression of power and authority. It can help to understand the origin of this piece of furniture.

In ancient times, the army of Rome was superior on the land, but they were powerless on the sea. In response to enemies, they built a fleet of ships and defeated their foes. In triumph, they cut off the prow (rostrum) of each captured ship and mounted it in the Forum. Speakers would mount these rostra to remind the listening Romans of the invincibility of their empire.

When you step to the podium, you should cloak yourself in that mantle of greatness.[11]

Just as your wardrobe ranges from formal to casual, so you need to be able to recognize the appropriateness of different adornments of speaking. The president would not deliver a State of the Union Address in shorts and a tee shirt and he would not deliver it without a podium. A project manager at a high-tech firm would not hold a weekly progress meeting with his engineers wearing a suit and tie, and neither should he stand at attention. He should be sitting or wandering as he talks because that stance is appropriate to the setting.

Chapter Nineteen

Voice, Audience, and Posture

When words are printed, there is not only ink on the paper but also white space. Typically, we double space between sentences, indent or double space between paragraphs, and start new pages for new chapters or new topics. In musical notation, there are not only notes but also rests, where no noise is made. Your spoken words demand the same.

When you are speaking, use silence as well as sound. Pause between ideas to alert your listeners to the fact that you are moving to something else. When you make a big point, give it time for emphasis and to let it sink in. Take the time to say what you have to say. If you have more material than time, do not go as deep into the triangle. Better to have your words fit elegantly and cleanly than to give the impression of an overstuffed sausage with too many words in too little time. More is not better; give them the ideas they need in the time you have.

Some people use "ums" as a space filler. These people cannot tolerate the proper silence between thoughts. Remember, no one will take away your right to speak if there is some dead air. Do not fill the spaces with the spoken equivalent of static. Phrases like "you know," and "like," similarly are to be eliminated.

For some people, "um" is a preface to each utterance. It is as though their voices need a warm-up before speaking. A related use of "um" is as a verbal punctuation mark. Such people say it to mark the end of a sentence. In any case, it always detracts from good speaking. If you listen to yourself, particularly when speaking in non-stressful situations, you will hear it and can, with the decision to do so, eliminate them.

Look at your newspaper. Notice the use of different fonts and, particularly, different font sizes. Headlines and bold print denote major points being introduced. These visual cues of size and boldness need to correspond to adding emphasis when you speak. Modulate your tone. Get louder for important points, normal for run of the mill ones, and use a quiet voice to really attract attention.

When Richard Burton was first asked to play the lead in *Camelot*, his initial reaction was that he could not sing. He then thought to himself, "I'm Welsh, my spoken voice is a song." In fact, listening to the recording, one can hear that Burton never actually sings, but speaks across the range of notes. While you may not be Richard Burton, you also can use your voice as an instrument.

Many people express anxiety by talking fast, on the unconscious theory that talking fast allows one to leave the danger zone sooner. This is a mistake. Slow down. If you go fast, it will tend to make you think you want to escape and make you nervous. Slow down, which will send a message to yourself that this is where you want to be.

Some people keep a proper pace until the end. They are like horses you rent for a trail ride at a resort. The nags amble along until they get near the stable, when the prospect of food, water, and getting you off their backs gets them all trotting quite briskly. Don't be like a cheap horse. Slow down near the end.

In general, remember that if you think that you are too dramatic, too slow, and too loud, you are possibly approaching the proper emphasis, speed, and volume.

Some people blush. Some of them worry about it a great deal. There are two simple secrets that can reduce or eliminate blushing for most people.

First of all, realize that blushing gains its power in inverse proportion to your fear of blushing. The more you worry about blushing, the more you will, and the more it will bother you. In the nineteenth century, a would-be blackmailer approached the Duke of Wellington, threatening to make certain embarrassing letters public. "Publish and be damned," replied the Iron Duke. With that, the rogue had no hold over the Field Marshall. If you say to yourself (and really mean it!) "So what if I blush," not only will it not bother you, but also you probably won't.

Second, most people can eliminate blushing by the simple strategy of trying to blush! Not only does trying to do it prove that you are not afraid of it, it also interferes with the blush mechanism. Blushing is regulated at a below-conscious level. Trying to do it not only is nearly impossible, but also, in fact, gets in the way of doing it at all.[12] So try to blush and thus keep your cheeks fair.

The make-up of the audience is another factor for many people, though when you think about it, this is absurd. Your job remains the same. People being there or not does not physically affect your task of telling a story.

A number of years ago, a famous pianist developed so severe a case of performance anxiety that he had to cease giving concerts. Eventually he sought the help of friends in overcoming his inhibition. They arranged for him to give a private performance, by invitation only, from behind a screen, where he could not see the audience. He was allowed to practice at the concert hall daily, getting the feel of playing the piano there, and he played magnificently to the empty facility. Finally, the evening of the concert arrived and he stepped to the piano to play. Behind his screen he could not see the audience, but felt their presence. He sat at the piano and broke out in tears, unable to perform a note.

His friends removed the screen, and he saw an empty hall. There had been no audience. It was not the people who incapacitated him. It had been his own mind.

When you talk, the people in the audience do not change your task, but they can change your perception. Several tips can help.

Some people find it hard to present to superiors, senior management, or authority figures. There you must remember the stories of the graduate students or new MBAs, who were giving their specialized, informed viewpoint. You must remember that you are an expert.

Presenting to peers can be a special problem.

Newbury Street in Boston is a *chic* shopping district, with stores ranging from international trend setters to small boutiques. One day, one of the smaller shops was having a tremendous sale. One shopper, glancing from her watch to the line for the changing room to the dress she was holding, said "What the heck, I don't know anybody here," whipped off her clothes, and tried on the dress she wanted. It fit and she bought it.

The same can apply to presenting. In front of strangers, you may feel less intimidated because you do not have to see them later. For others, familiar faces can be comforting. In either case, remember that you have a presenting *persona*. In front of friends, you are not your usual self but rather "the expert." You are not relating as one of the group but as the authority. Assuming this authority is a difficult but important part of success. If you are one of the troops, you will not advance.

The size of the group affects many people in various ways. Some prefer small groups, others like large ones. Almost everyone misunderstands the effects of group size.

People who study group dynamics find that groups change character from small group to large group at about 15 to 20 members. Smaller is a small group; larger is a large group.

Talking with one person, you have a single target audience. When talking to two or three individuals, you are dealing with two or three targets. The task is slightly different, but manageable. If the group grows somewhat, the individual members can be thought of as clustering, so a dozen individuals can be seen to behave like two or three small groups, and so the dozen can be treated like two or three individuals. The process remains the same. Small groups are like a small number of individuals, with mini-groups in place of single people.

When the group gets over fifteen or twenty, however, something interesting happens. It becomes a large group. And the dynamics of a large group are such that it is too big to treat with different factions. Instead, dealing with a large group is like dealing with a single individual. The factions within a large group are akin to the different thoughts and feelings of one person. The secret of managing to address a large group, whether twenty-five or twenty-five million, is to realize that you can treat all large groups the same. Think of the group as a single entity.

An important element in feeling secure when presenting is to feel at home. Our Neanderthal ancestors needed to feel safe in a cave before they could relax. You need to do the same to be comfortable presenting. You need to make everyplace your home field.

When a dog moves into a new environment, the first thing it does is to drink lots of water and go around the area "marking" its territory. When athletes play for the first time at a new field, they frequently spit more than usual. (They sometimes do more than spit before the game.) You need to do a less crude version of the same. When you are going to present in an unfamiliar place, go there early, if possible. Walk around. Touch corners, leaving fingerprints as your mark. Give yourself the reassuring feeling that this is your territory. If you cannot get there early to walk around, instead, when you arrive, take a few minutes to look around. Look in the corners and ends of the space. See what is there. Make it feel safe and secure. This is no longer enemy territory but your territory.

The way you dress and present yourself gives a clear set of non-verbal but powerful messages.

Basically, if you dress like your audience, you will be recognized as a member of their clan. If you dress differently, you will be seen at a gut level as a member of another clan.

There is no one right way to dress. The important thing is to send out the message you wish to send out. If you want to appear to be a serious investor, dress like one. If you want to come across as a boffin or high-tech wizard, wear jeans and a tee shirt. I have suggested to software start-ups who are meeting with VCs that they send two people, one in a suit and tie to discuss the business plan and numbers, the other in shorts, sandals, and tee shirt (and a neat ponytail, if possible) to discuss the technical side of their product.

Your posture also sends important messages to your listeners. The natural stance of a person is relaxed, with weight distributed on both feet, and a general mild bend of the joints. (Figure 1) To be rigid is unnatural and not only looks tense but also makes you feel nervous.

Figure 1

Figure 2

To put a hand in a pocket (Figure 2) is to send a message of casual demeanor, which may be appropriate in some settings and not others.

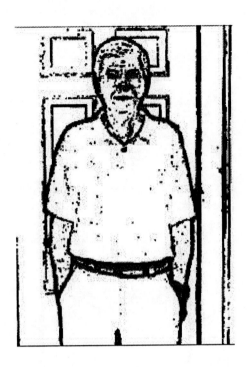

Figure 3

Both hands in pockets (Figure 3) indicates an extreme of casual attitude.

Figure 4

When Michael Caine wanted to portray an English general, he studied Prince Phillip to learn how to express authority with body language. He noted that the prince kept his hands behind his back all the time (Figure 4). The message is that if anything needs to be picked up or carried, someone will do it, but it won't be the prince.

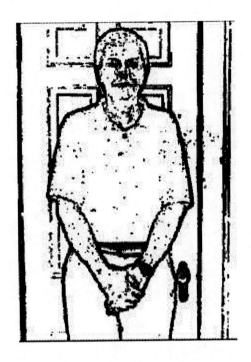

Figure 5

The above posture (Figure 5) should never be seen unless you are defending a free kick in a soccer game.

Finally, remember to use your hands (Figure 6). They can be an invaluable way of adding emphasis, of marking points as you make them, and conducting the flow of the talk like a symphony conductor with his baton.

Figure 6

One of the greatest orators of the ancient world was Cicero. When Augustus had him killed after the assassination of Julius Caesar, he ordered that not only should his head be stuck on a stake, as was customary, but also that his hands should be on stakes on either side, as his tongue would be too lonely without its companions.

Just remember to keep your hands moving in rhythm with your speech, not flying off like birds with lives of their own. Also, keep them away from your face and especially your mouth.

Finally, remember that as well as you know your topic, as often as you have discussed it, perhaps as often as you have delivered this very speech, you have to make it fresh. It is new to your listeners and they need to hear your best effort.

When I took my family to Disney world, we went on the spaceship to Mars ride. A live woman flight attendant and rocket pilot played by a robot were the hosts on board the ship. The flesh and blood woman was bored and gave her lines by rote, flat and stale. The robot, on the other hand, delivered his part with all the enthusiasm of his very first flight. He was the more alive of the two. You need to avoid the boredom of that woman without becoming a robot.

When *My Fair Lady* played for year after year on Broadway, Rex Harrison and Julie Andrews played the same roles day after day, month after month. They could have gotten stale, but if they had, the show would have closed. What they had to remember every day was that in the audience was a couple from Iowa who were seeing their first Broadway play, and they owed it to them to give their best.

Throughout it all, you need to remember that there are frequently different ways of making your point. Just be sure that you are choosing the way that conveys the message you wish to deliver.

Chapter Twenty

When Do You Start Talking?

You know how to begin your talk, but when do you actually begin it?

Does this book begin with the cover? Perhaps with the Library of Congress information page? Or with the title and author page? Take this book, for example. Where does it actually start? The opening words of text are

> "Talking is natural. It really is.
> "Most children have begun to speak…"

That is where the book really begins. This is where I first made contact with the reader. Earlier parts, a bad title or perhaps an ugly cover, could have influenced you never to open it up, and so you would have never read a word of content, but the opening lines of text are our first real interaction.

What about when you are going to give a talk. When does it actually start?

Think of a journal article's format. Typically, the first page of an article looks something like this:

Name of the Journal

Title of the Article

By Author

Author's job title

Abstract: This is a one-paragraph summary of the contents of the article that allows the reader to decide whether it is worth reading the whole thing

This is the opening sentence of the article. The text continues from this point.

Notice the different parts and see how they relate to a talk you might give. Notice particularly the similarities and differences when you are introduces compared to when you do not have an emcee.

In the case of a symposium or series of talks, the journal title equates to the name of the conference. If you are in a regular meeting at work, the title is not named but is understood by everyone.

The title of the article is the topic of your talk. When you are introduced by someone else, whether merely by name or with a biographical list of your achievements, these are merely the author line plus the author's job title lines. When you have to introduce yourself, whether by name ("Good morning, I'm Sean Kelly,") or by function ("I will be your guide on this journey,") this also is merely the author line. Giving your credentials is the job title line. While it is the first connection, it is not your carefully crafted opening. On the frequent occasions when your listeners know you, this line is understood and not mentioned.

Sometimes, though more often not, it is useful to give a summary abstract of your talk. While this frequently is an invitation not to listen further, it can be useful in two situations. The first is when only a fraction of the audience needs to listen to this next section in any detail, so you are allowing them to sort themselves out according to need to know. The second is when the topic is detailed or technical and requires a mental shift by the audience. "I am going to tell you about the technical specifications of out prototype."

Now you know when you are starting. So what about the moments before you finally start?

Chapter Twenty-one

Just Before You Say Your First Word

You have prepared your talk vertically and horizontally, you have your opening and closing designed, and you understand who you are in the process of presenting. You know how to go from preparation to performance, how to transition from the first pillar, knowledge of content and technique, to the second, knowledge of yourself. You have moved from the well-organized knowledge that is inside you to the equally important sense of who you are. You know that neither alone is sufficient. The combination of the two is required for excellence. Now you are just about ready to speak up. It is now only seconds before you begin to present.

How do you spend these final minutes and seconds?

When you are going to speak, whether it is a well-planned major presentation or an impromptu remark at a meeting, you are aware of the content you bring to the situation. When you are there, on the spot, you have as much knowledge as you have. You are as prepared as you are. Preparation time is over. Rehearsals are a thing of the past. It's Showtime.

In Chapter Four we discussed the range of things you know and do not know and the importance of focusing on the former. Now, we take it one step further. You must come to grips with the fact that you only know what you brought to this situation.

I did some work with an investment firm in Boston and the dress code was business casual. The following week I was scheduled to work at their Wall Street office. As I was taking the Water Shuttle down the East River from La Guardia to the tip of Manhattan, it occurred to me that the New York dress code might be more formal than the Boston rules. In fact, it was not unlikely that it would be. But there I was, at seven-fifteen in the morning, on a boat, wearing khaki slacks, a blue Oxford cloth shirt, and loafers. My nearest tie, much less suit, was a plane ride away in Boston.

I realized that no matter what anyone else was wearing, I would be the guy in business casual on Wall Street that Monday. I did not have other clothing. If I was not properly dressed, I could do nothing about it that day. I could know to dress more formally the next day, but that Monday I had what I had.[13]

The same applies to your preparation. You have what you brought. If it seems scanty, next time you can prepare better. Today you must go with what you have. This is not a choice or an option; it is hard reality.

That means that any thoughts of guilt or regret are not useful. In fact, they are poisonous. They make you less able to present what you do know. Any thoughts of wishing you knew more need to be met with the response, "I'll think of that later. Right now I'm busy focusing on what I do know."

So there you are, prepared to present, whether in a few minutes or a few seconds. What are you going to do? Here is where you need to unlearn much of what seems natural and develop a new way of spending those final moments.

You need to learn to trust yourself.

You have been in the process of learning that you can trust yourself. Hold on to that trust for a few minutes more.

In order to learn to handle the final minutes and seconds before you actually begin, let's look at a familiar, dreaded, presentation experience: the introduction.

Everyone has had the experience of sitting in a circle, part of a group of people, when the leader asks the participants to introduce themselves. This makes many people very uncomfortable. Understanding why this is so and how to combat it can reveal how to overcome the problems most people encounter just before beginning. After all, telling your name is an example of a simple speech.

In our introduction example, the one who goes first has the easiest task; the degree of difficulty is directly correlated with how long you have to wait. The last position is the hardest. The reason is that most people do the absolute worst thing while they are waiting. They think about saying their names. They do this before it is their turn. This has two results, both bad.

First, to think about saying your name is to produce an impulse to do so. You think about saying your name and it wants to come out. But it is not your turn, so you have to stop yourself. You are saying/ not saying your name. You simultaneously are pushing to speak and pulling to hold yourself back. Think of sitting in a car with your left foot pushing down the brake pedal while your right floors the gas. The car may not move, just as you may be silent, but it is not happy and neither are you. The result is opposing forces building in intensity, a sort of mental isometric exercise that results in tension. And we know that tension translates into anxiety.

Second, this inward focus on saying/not saying your name directs your attention inward. You begin to pay attention to what is going on inside. (You might in fact want to try to do this right now, as you read, because reading about inward focus can produce the same effect.) How does your mouth feel? Is it dry? Is there too much saliva? How about your palms? Are they moist or dry? What about your armpits? Even more frightening, perhaps you can feel your heart beating. Things must be really bad if your heart is beating so loudly that you can feel it. You must be very nervous indeed.

And when you think of yourself as nervous, you are.

In fact, there is nothing terribly surprising about any of these sensations. You can observe the moisture state of body parts at any time. You can always feel your heart beat if you pay attention.[14] Ordinarily you have your attention directed out into the world around you. That is why you are not aware of the status of these symptoms. If your heart were to stop beating you would become aware of that instantly! The beating is normal. If it is faster than usual, you have initiated a touch of fight or flight, and you know now how counterproductive that is.

The problem comes from directing your attention inward. Doing so makes you feel like the mythical ostrich, hiding his head in the sand in the face of danger. Satchel Paige said, "Don't look back. Something might be gaining in you." But this sort of outlook implies that there is danger behind you. Are you running because you are frightened or are you frightened because you are running? Since you are not looking outward, it feels as if there might be, or even must be, something bad out there.

The solution in the name circle is to direct your attention outward. Listen to each person say his or her name. Pay attention and try to remember each name. Do not even think about saying your name. When it is not time to say your name, do not even think about it. Why think about doing what you are not going to do?

When the time finally does come for you to introduce yourself, I guarantee that your name will be there, waiting for you. You will know it. I have never heard of anyone having to take out a driver's license or library card because they could not remember their own name. You really do know it.

Focus your attention on what is happening outside of yourself in the present, whether you are waiting to introduce yourself or to begin a presentation, and you will see that all is well. You are safe. There is no danger. You will relax because you will not be stressing yourself by trying to both do and inhibit doing simultaneously. You will know that you can wait until it is time to speak and you will know that your content will be there waiting for you.

You must not rehearse while waiting to begin.

You need to trust that you arrived ready to speak and that there is nothing more to do but wait. You need to remember that all you can do now is to diminish the state of readiness you brought with you into the room. It is all there, waiting for you. When you start to talk, it will flow forth, each bit leading smoothly to the next.

If you try to test yourself, "to see if you are ready," no good can come of it. The very questioning will erode your confidence. There is nothing more you can do now anyway.

Relax. Pay attention to what is going on outside of you. Give yourself the confidence boost of not mentally scrambling for one last run-through. Not going over it will reassure you that you do not need to do so. Focus on a feeling of relaxed confidence.

So now you know how to wait until it is time to begin to talk. So how do you start?

When it is time to begin, you need to launch yourself strongly and confidently. If you need to clear your throat, do it in advance. Any nose blowing, sorting through notes and papers,[15] adjusting your clothes, licking your lips, or anything else that is not part of your talk needs to be gotten out of the way in advance. If you have any "Ums," get them out of your system beforehand. Any, "Well, I sort of was thinking about maybe saying…" has no place here.

Think of an Olympic runner in the starting blocks. When the starter's pistol fires, he does not say, "Wait a minute. My laces are untied." When the waiting is over, when you are about to start talking, you need to be ready to plunge right in.

You may give a perfunctory prefatory phrase ("Good afternoon,") as a signal that you are about to begin to talk, if you wish. If you do, understand that it not really your talk but rather is a signal, like lowering the lights at Symphony Hall, that indicates that the audience should sit down and shut up, because you are about to start and you demand attention. That's right, demand. If you get up hoping to gain respect and attention, you have already conceded that you are not yet worthy of it. Your initial demeanor and presentation has to communicate to your listeners that you are worthy of their interest, that they will do well to be attentive. After all, if you do not think they should pay attention, why should they?

Whether you use the attention getting phrase or not, pause for a moment before saying your first word. Give them the opportunity to focus attention on you. More important, by giving a moment of silence, you make them eager to hear what your first words will be. Give them a second or two of anticipation to hone interest.

Then and only then do you deliver your crafted opening lines.

Chapter Twenty-Two

Talking Naturally

Congratulations. You are ready to present to anyone, anywhere, at any time.

Now it's time to begin.

You know what your first words are. Say them proudly and confidently.

Stay in the moment. Know that as you finish one point, the next will be there, waiting for you, like the final digits in your phone number.

Remember who you are, what you are saying, and why you are saying it. Remember who your audience is.

Most of all, have confidence that because you know both the pillars of success, you can just do it, rather than think about it.

You have restored an ability that you had as a child. You can talk. You need never lose it again. It's yours. Keep it forever.

Talking is, once again, natural.

NOTES

[1] Two parameters define the limits of any potential success: the strength of the opponent and the absolute limit of your own potential. In competition, the caliber of the opposition has a direct bearing upon the outcome. A round of golf good enough to win a club tournament would probably not be good enough to win at Augusta. Further, your ability to succeed is limited by your ability. You cannot be better than your best. It is not bad luck or lack of confidence that prevents golfers from getting an eagle on every hole. On the PGA tour, most, if not all, of the players know the technique to hit a golf ball and many of them have the right mental approach. Some of them are just better than others. Similarly, women's tees are further forward not because most women do not know how to play the game as well as men but rather because men are, on average, bigger, stronger, and so tend to be able to hit the ball farther.

[2] An ancient joke illustrates this. Patient: "Will I be able to play the piano after the cast comes off?" Doctor: "Yes, of course." Patient: "That's odd. I couldn't play it before I broke my arm."

[3] This book gives you both a way of organizing knowledge, the first pillar of success, and techniques to fortify your sense of self, the second. For those who decide to use alternate methods of data management, the second part works independently of whether you use the former. There are more than one good ways to do anything, including knowledge management.

[4] Feynman, Richard P. *Six Easy Pieces.* Reading, MA: Addison-Wesley, 1995.

[5] Note that just because you are trying to bring them to your destination does not mean they will actually agree to end up there. And particularly note that your failure to persuade them does not mean you gave a poor presentation. Suppose you were trying to convince a die-hard Red Sox fan to root for the Yankees. No matter how well you argued your case, you would never get agreement. And sometimes you will persuade people despite making your argument ineptly. How difficult would it be to convince a Yankee fan that he roots for the greatest dynasty in baseball history? At the conclusion of *The Music Man*, the parents of River City saw and heard their children's marching band with eyes and ears of love and thought they were great, despite the objective reality.

[6] In general, the division frequently can be conceptualized as a split between those who need to know what and those who need to also know how. The patient needs to know what operation he needs, the surgeon needs to know how to perform it.

[7] In my talk that I described last chapter, where there was an introduction, five points, and a conclusion, my basic organization was even simpler. There were three points in my horizontal organization. The first was the introduction. The second was "case studies." Under this heading were the examples, each of which served as a sub-point. The third was the conclusion. Because this was so simple, in practice I thought of it as having the greater number of points.

[8] Early Beatle albums included covers of songs originally recorded by Chuck Berry, Buddy Holly, Carl Perkins, and others. They did not sound like the American originals.

[9] A subtler but important issue involves copying yourself. As noted previously, sometimes you need to give the same basic speech to very different audiences, such as factory workers and the board of directors of your company. Just as you should not try to be someone else when giving his or her talk, so you should not try to give exact copies of one talk in every situation. Think of how talented musicians record different versions of the same song. It is not that the earlier was bad, but rather that they wanted to give a different feel and texture to the music. The differences are often quite marked in studio versus live recordings. Another noteworthy example is the comparison between the original and "unplugged" recordings of "Layla," by Eric Clapton.

[10] It is possible to do this with a simple game like tic-tac-toe. There are only nine possible first moves, (three considering that the symmetry of the game surface allows rotation to decrease the real number of possible positions) and eight (or five or two) possible responses to each of these. It does not take long to figure out all the possibilities in such a limited field.

[11] An elaboration of its use is to step away from the podium for a moment to dramatically say that you are giving an informal aside, then return to the formal position of the speaker's place.

[12] The exception is if you try to do it by thinking about something embarrassing. Just as thinking about something exciting will raise your heart rate, so thinking about embarrassing subjects can cause a blush. The secret is simply to try to blush out of context.

[13] On arrival, I immediately saw that the New York office was an even more casual version of business dress than Boston. However, if they had all been in regulation Brooks Brothers tailored wool suits, I still needed to be accepting the reality of my Brooks Brothers casual attire. If I were to focus on how out of place I looked, I would not have been able to do a good job working with the senior vice-president of the firm.

[14] Many people doubt this until they try it. Close your eyes and focus your attention on feeling your heartbeat. You may first notice it as a pulse in your head, neck, or extremities. If you continue to sit quietly, ignoring other stimuli, you will feel it clearly. Because it is always there as a background noise, you very early on learn to ignore it, under ordinary circumstances. The fact that you can observe it merely means you are listening, not that it is somehow worse.

[15] This does not mean that you should not use props dramatically and effectively. For example, an attorney about to cross-examine a witness might choose to begin with a moment of silence as she looks at a transcript of earlier testimony. She is not really doing some last-minute preparation, but rather is focusing the jury's attention on the fact that there is written rebuttal of what the witness had said.

Printed in the United States
61847LVS00003B/139-153